D0443400

Tips and tricks from

## *Ask the Past*

### *How to Cure a Headache, ninth century*
"Take some earth, touch your breast three times and say: My head hurts, why does it hurt? It does not hurt."

### *How to Grow a Beard, 1544*
"Take honeybees in quantity and dry them in a basket by the fire, then make a powder of them, which you moisten with olive oil, and with this ointment, dab several times the place where you would like to have hair, and you will see miracles."

### *How to Dress for Bathing, 1881*
"Flannel is the best material for a bathing costume, and gray is regarded as the most suitable color…an oilskin cap to protect the hair from the water, and merino socks to match the dress, complete the costume."

### *How to Pack for a Journey, 1480*
"[A traveler] should carry with him two bags: one very full of patience, the other containing two hundred Venetian ducats, or at least one hundred and fifty."

# Ask the Past

*Pertinent and Impertinent*
*Advice from Yesteryear*

~

## ELIZABETH P. ARCHIBALD

hachette
BOOKS

NEW YORK   BOSTON

Hachette Books
Hachette Book Group
1290 Avenue of the Americas
New York, NY 10104

www.HachetteBookGroup.com

Printed in the United States of America

RRD-C

First Edition: May 2015
10   9   8   7   6   5   4   3   2   1

Hachette Books is a division of Hachette Book Group, Inc.
The Hachette Books name and logo are trademarks of Hachette Book Group, Inc.

The publisher is not responsible for websites (or their content) that are not owned by the publisher.

Library of Congress Cataloging-in-Publication date.

Archibald, Elizabeth, 1951–
    Ask the past : pertinent and impertinent advice from yesteryear / Elizabeth P. Archibald. — First edition.
        pages cm
    Includes bibliographical references.     *5652   5214   06/15*
    ISBN 978-0-316-29889-6 (hardback) — ISBN 978-1-4789-8711-6 (audio download) — ISBN 9780316298872 (ebook)   1. Curiosities and wonders.   2. Curiosities and wonders—Early works to 1800.   3. Conduct of life—History.   4. Etiquette—Early works to 1800.   5. Handbooks, vade-mecums, etc.   I. Title.
    AG241.A84 2015
    032.01—dc23

                                2015007670

# *Introduction*

"Find a way to steal bees" was not on my to-do list, but sometimes the bee-stealing technique finds you. Seeking materials for a new seminar I was teaching at Johns Hopkins University's Peabody Institute on the history of how-to manuals, I found myself turning pages in the rare books collection at the George Peabody Library.

My investigations yielded some remarkable finds: locally printed nineteenth-century palmistry manuals, a vermin-destroying compendium authored by a royal ratcatcher, an 1884 book called *How to Get Strong* whose merits were advertised by the disembodied biceps on the book's spine. And nestled between techniques for salvaging tainted venison and drunk-proofing yourself by sipping salad oil, there it was: "How to steal bees." By then I knew that these instructions deserved a wider audience.

I began posting morsels of historical advice on a blog for the amusement of my friends and colleagues. Soon inquiries began to arrive from around the world. "Dear Past," they said. "How should I wash my hair?" "How can I remove a stain?" "What should I pack for my vacation?" (The answers, in no particular order: cured tongue, mushrooms, and lizards.[1])

The advice contained in this book is a rowdy assortment, preserved in libraries, curated by whimsy. Yet the landscape

---

1 See pages 68, 129, and 29.

of instruction that comes into view has some surprisingly
clear features, and, as keeper of serendipitous advice, I want to
outline them here. Most fundamentally, the fact that all of these
suggestions survive in books means that authors thought they
were worth recording and scribes or printers thought they were
worth transmitting. Thus, for the historian, sixteenth-century
advice about belching is valuable data about the history of civility,
but also about the history of books and written instruction.

These texts also share certain goals. A how-to text is a kind of
contract between author and reader. The author gives instructions,
and the reader follows them. The author emerges from this
contract with esteem and royalties, and the reader emerges with
devastating abs, a cake in the shape of a wombat, and a flawlessly
constructed IKEA dresser, or so goes the theory. This contract is
implied in the preface to one collection of clever tips from 1579:
the author promises readers that "their money is not lost," for they
will save twenty times the book's price through its thrifty tips; as
he puts it, "The paines and trauell hethertoo is mine:/the gaine
and pleasure hence forth will be thine."[2]

How-to manuals offer possibility. They assure readers that
overcoming a limitation of nature or society does not require
divine intervention, inborn privilege, or years of practice—just
a clever technique, and perhaps the gall of a weasel. Consider
Antonius Arena's 1530 dance manual, which cautions that "the
ladies...ridicule and make great sport of those who do not dance
well and who do not know the steps, and say, 'Those people are
yokels'...Kings, queens, counts and barons all dance themselves
and command others to dance."[3] Be honest: you are a yokel. But

---

2 Thomas Lupton, *A Thousand Notable Things, of Sundry Sortes* (London, 1579), title
page.

3 John Guthrie and Marino Zorzi, ed. and tr., in "Rules of Dancing by Antonius
Arena," *Dance Research* 4, no. 2 (1986), 8–9.

read on, and you will become suave and even "learn the dances in which you may bestow prolonged kisses."[4]

This is part of a long and helpful tradition of texts that aim to make you courteous, urbane, and civil—all of which mean, essentially, "not a yokel." (*Curialitas* is the attribute of someone at home in a *curia*, a court, and thus courteous; *urbanitas* is the quality of an urban dweller; and *civilitas* is associated with the *civitas*, or city.) Medieval texts like Daniel of Beccles's *Urbanus magnus* or *Liber urbani* (*The Book of the Civilized Man*) were already noting important principles of courtesy, such as not attacking an enemy who is squatting to defecate.

By the sixteenth century, courtesy advice was all around, aided by the rise in literacy and circulation of texts that came with the printing press. The great Dutch humanist Erasmus of Rotterdam composed his *De civilitate morum puerilium* (*On Civility of Children's Manners*) in 1530 on the brilliant premise that schoolboys could learn farting protocol and Latin from a single book.[5] In Italy, where court culture flourished, Baldassare Castiglione's 1528 *Il cortegiano* (*The Courtier*) emerged as one of the most influential Italian literary texts; the dialogue explores qualities of the ideal courtier (for instance his tasteful clothing). And Giovanni della Casa's *Galateo* cautions that a badly told joke gives the impression that "someone very fat with an enormous butt is dancing and hopping about in a tight-fitting vest."[6] Courtesy manuals (in particular those of Erasmus and Della Casa) were widely imitated, offering the promise of civility to a newly expanded reading public.

If such texts held out the possibility of self-fashioning—that is, of transforming from a yokel into a sophisticated and urbane

---

4 Ibid., 26.

5 See page 9.

6 See page 125.

courtier—another type of popular how-to manual promised to help fashion the world around you. The collections of "secrets of nature," "conceits," and "marvels" that captivated early modern European readers emerged from a much older tradition of arcane Hellenistic alchemical lore, although one would not guess it from their preoccupation with bedbug destruction and pranks involving meat. One of the earliest surviving European books of "secrets," attested from the ninth century but with a core of ancient material, includes techniques for coloring glass, hides, and ink; cleaning silver; and constructing a battering ram. One suspects "The Recipe for the Most Gold" was a selling point: "it will cause wonder," promises the text.[7] Even if that wonder was only of the "I wonder where my Most Gold is" variety, a failed alchemist could keep reading and console himself by mixing up a nice batch of French soap or sesame candy.

Even more recent collections dressed themselves up with a little Eau de Antiquity. When medieval European scholars began to seek ancient scientific and medical knowledge in Arabic texts, Aristotle (known simply as "The Philosopher") was on the agenda. Hitching a ride among the Aristotelian works was an encyclopedic patchwork of Arabic political, medical, and astrological lore known as *Kitāb Sirr al-Asrār* (*Book of the Secret of Secrets*, or *Secretum secretorum* in its Latin translation). Paradoxically but predictably, the top-secret secrets of "Aristotle" became a European best-seller, overshadowing Aristotle's actual works by a long shot. The practice of name-dropping The Philosopher in order to legitimize a text continued for centuries, as illustrated by the wildly popular 1684 sex manual known as *Aristotle's Masterpiece* or *The Works of Aristotle, the Famous Philosopher.* (One imagines the conversations:

---

7 Cyril Stanley Smith and John G. Hawthorne, tr., in "Mappae Clavicula: A Little Key to the World of Medieval Techniques," *Transactions of the American Philosophical Society*, n.s. 64, no. 4 (1974), 30.

"What's that you're reading?" "Oh, just the works of Aristotle, the famous philosopher.")

Were medieval and early modern readers suspicious of the fact that the ancient philosophers peddled tips for tooth whitening and stain removal rather than transcendence and aurifaction? Undoubtedly—but the mundane orientation of these texts hardly detracted from their appeal. And as the printing industry developed, a new group of professionals—printers and professional writers—began to market books to the newly expanded reading public. Little pamphlets of everyday advice proliferated, like the *Dificio di ricette*, a 1525 collection of secrets assembled by an Italian printer who correctly assessed the reading public's desire to know how to grow a beard and burn candles underwater.

The mania for advice also promoted the success of "Alessio Piemontese" (often identified with the humanist Girolamo Ruscelli), whose book of secrets was first published in 1555.[8] Less than fifty years later, it had seen seventy editions in eight languages. The preface reads a bit like an infomercial:

> I have wandered and trauailed abroad in the world the space of xxvii yeares, to the intent to acquaint my self with al sortes of learned and discret men. By the which diligence and curiositie, I haue learned many goodly secretes, not alonely of men of great knowledge and profound learning, & noble men, but also of poore women artificers, peysantes, and al sortes of men.[9]

---

8 See William Eamon, *Science and the Secrets of Nature: Books of Secrets in Medieval and Early Modern Culture* (Princeton, 1994), 147–55.

9 *The Secretes of the reuerend Maister Alexis of Piemont*, tr. William Ward (London, 1562).

The promotion of "poore women artificers" as sources for secrets creates quite a different effect than name-dropping Aristotle for legitimacy, highlighting a general trend away from reliance on ancient authority and toward interest in experimentation. Collections of secrets often append the word *Probatus* ("tested" or "proven") to their techniques, or explain with a brief anecdote how effective they know the technique to be. ("I knewe a man that was marueilous grosse...that with this medicine tooke away his grosnes," says Thomas Lupton of a slim-fast regimen.[10])

The popular appetite for secrets gave rise to a category of experimenters known as "professors of secrets," a title that evokes Hogwarts glamor but belies a reality of Counter-Reformation persecution. Among them was Giambattista della Porta, whose fascination with natural magic was not applauded by the Church. While his fascination with oddities of nature perhaps verged on the unhealthy, Della Porta's "natural magic" is more mundane than it sounds: growing a peach in the shape of a human head by slipping it inside a mold, for instance, counts as natural magic. (It also counts as creepy, in case you were wondering.)

Growing a face on a peach may not be the pinnacle of intellectual inquiry or experimental science, but it is a good illustration of the significance of "books of secrets" and the flourishing of how-to manuals in general. Just as courtesy manuals made the rules of courtly life available for anyone with access to their advice, books of secrets offered control over nature to any and all readers.

If the advice worked, that is. Did readers believe in the efficacy of remedies and techniques that appear highly doubtful to modern eyes? Consider, for instance, a 1581 method for walking on water. With two little plates attached to his feet, the walker is instructed to stride across the water "with a certaine boldnesse

---

10 See page 43.

and lightnesse of the body." If the technique does not win your confidence, you are not alone: a snarky contemporary reader noted in the margin of one copy of the book that "if you do sink you shall be sure to doe soe upon the water."[11]

This little jibe might suggest that the manuals deliver less than they promise, but they also deliver more. How-to books do not simply outline the easiest path to a desired result. Some advice is really the occasion for a literary romp; this is the case for poetic extravaganzas like Ovid's *Ars amatoria* (although its smooth pickup moves—pretend to brush some dust off her garment!— might still play well). But even texts of humbler literary pretensions could serve purposes other than serious transmission of a toothpaste recipe. Authors of how-to manuals recognized the sometimes ridiculous conventions of their form and played with them: consider, for instance, a parody recipe included in a medieval cookbook promising "a good dish for somebody who likes to eat it" that includes pints of sweat, pebble grease, goldfinch heels, and flies' feet.[12] Admittedly, historical distance makes it more difficult to distinguish between parody and sincerity when earwax is prescribed for eye problems and the gall of an eel is a typical ingredient. Still, how-to manuals contain a healthy dose of practical jokes (the notorious fart candle) and silly anecdotes ("to make a cat piss out a fire"), suggesting that they were as much pleasure reading as reference manual.

In that spirit, I offer you these pieces of instruction. Although I still expect you to try them all.

---

11 Thomas Hill, *A Briefe and Pleasant Treatise, Intituled, Naturall and Artificiall Conclusions* (London, 1581); see page 21. The annotated copy is from the Huntington Library and Art Gallery, San Marino, CA .

12 Melitta Weiss Adamson, "The Games Cooks Play: Non-Sense Recipes and Practical Jokes in Medieval Literature," in *Food in the Middle Ages: A Book of Essays,* ed. Melitta Weiss Adamson (New York, 1995), 179.

# A Note about the Texts

The texts collected here were inspired by my own interests in medieval and early modern European education and the history of the book, and this has determined their chronological and geographical scope (from late antiquity through the early modern period, with a few diverting excursions beyond, and almost entirely European). The Past is, of course, much more expansive than what appears here, and I encourage all initiatives to Ask It.

By presenting the texts without a rigid chronological or topical structure, I am following the example of many of their sources. For one thing, it is difficult to assign material to a single time period when useful advice simply stayed around: Pliny the Elder proposed a garland of violets as a hangover remedy, and the recommendation still pops up now and again, probably to remain in circulation until the blessed day when mankind discovers a truly effective hangover cure. The excerpts here do not represent the first time their advice appeared in print (or in a manuscript), but they do represent a time when readers encountered it; by the same logic, the dates provided are those of the editions I consulted and not necessarily first editions (although their dates, along with information about translations, are provided in the notes).

The miscellaneous nature of the material, too, follows the example of its sources. A topical arrangement of material would be anachronistic, reflecting current divisions of knowledge rather than periods when music was a branch of math, say, and cookbooks told you how to condition your hair. And consider Thomas Lupton's *A Thousand Notable Things* (1579), which gathers ancient and recent lore on all subjects, offering it up in delightful disarray. In the space of a page, a reader can marvel at:

- a technique to heal a wound with sugar and a pat of butter
- a story about a child the author met in June 1577 who "dyd eate the woollen sleeues that were on her armes, besydes that she dyd eate a gloue"
- a remedy for baldness (mouse dung, burned wasps, hazelnuts, vinegar)
- a foolproof way to make frogs stop croaking with a candle

As justification for my own jumbled organization, I cannot improve on Lupton's own preface to his thousand notable things:

Perhappes you will meruell, that I haue not placed them in better order, and that thinges of like matter are not ioygned together. Truely there are so many of so diuerse and sundry sortes and contrary effectes, that it could not be altogether obserued. And in my iudgement through the straungenesse and varietie of matter, it will be more desirously and delightfully read: knowing we are made of such a moulde, that delicate Daintinesse delightes vs much: but we loathe to bee fed too long with one foode: And that long wandring in straunge, peasant and contrary places, will lesse wery vs, then short trauell in often troden ground.[1]

Happy wandring.

1 Lupton A₃v.

# Ask the Past

Giac. Franco f.

# *How to Impress Girls at a Dance*

~

## 1538

"Friend, when you are dancing, be careful not to belch, for if you belch then you will be a real pig. Furthermore never fart when you are dancing; grit your teeth and compel your arse to hold back the fart…Do not have a dripping nose and do not dribble at the mouth. No woman desires a man with rabies. And refrain from spitting before the maidens, because that makes one sick and even revolts the stomach. If you spit or blow your nose or sneeze, remember to turn your head away after the spasm; and remember not to wipe your nose with your fingers; do it properly with a white handkerchief. Do not eat either leeks or onions because they leave an unpleasant odour in the mouth."

Antonius Arena, *Leges dansandi*

The female heart is an enigma, but let's just say that rabies and intestinal gas aren't doing you any favors on the dance floor.

.

1

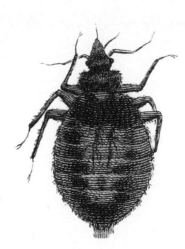

# How to Kill Bedbugs

~

## 1777

"Spread Gun,powder, beaten small, about the crevices of your bedstead; fire it with a match, and keep the smoak in; do this for an hour or more, and keep the room close several hours."

*The Complete Vermin-Killer*

Oh, you want to kill the bedbugs *without* reducing your bed to a smoking pile of debris? Clearly you have never had bedbugs.

# How to Tell If Someone Is
# or Is Not Dead

~

## c. 1380

"Moreover, if there is any doubt as to whether a person is or is not dead, apply lightly roasted onion to his nostrils, and if he be alive, he will immediately scratch his nose."

Johannes de Mirfield, *Breviarium Bartholomei*

Don't bother checking for a pulse—the onion reflex is the only reliable sign of life.

4

# *How to Treat Freshmen*

~

## 1495

"Statute Forbidding Any One to Annoy or Unduly Injure the
*Beani* [Freshmen]. Each and every one attached to this university
is forbidden to offend with insult, torment, harass, drench with
water or urine, throw on or defile with dust or any filth, mock by
whistling, cry at them with a terrifying voice, or dare to molest
in any way whatsoever physically or severely, any, who are called
*beani*, in the market, streets, courts, colleges and living houses,
or any place whatsoever, and particularly in the present college,
when they have entered in order to matriculate or are leaving
after matriculation."

Leipzig University Statute

Note that duly injuring the freshmen is still an option.

# How to Chat with a Woman

~

## C. 1180S

"After greeting the lady, the man should allow a moment or two to elapse to permit the woman to speak first, should she so desire. If the woman herself starts the conversation, you will have good cause for satisfaction, assuming that you are not a fluent conversationalist, because her comment will give you plenty of topics for discussion…But if the woman delays too long before beginning to speak, you must after a short pause cleverly break into conversation. First make some casual observation with an amusing point, or praise her native region or her family or her person."

Andreas Capellanus, *De amore*

> Man: Hello.
> Woman: Hi.
> Man: …
> Woman: …
> Man: You're from Aquitaine, right? Aquitaine is so great.
> Woman: …
> Man: I like your tunic.
> Woman: …

*How to Sweet-Talk Your Lady, 1656,* page 210.

# How to Fart

~

## 1530

"Some teach that a boy should keep in the gas of his belly by compressing his buttocks. But it is not civil to become ill while you are trying to seem polite. If it is possible to leave, let him do it alone, but if not, follow the ancient proverb: Hide the fart with a cough."

Desiderius Erasmus, *De civilitate morum puerilium*

Erasmus, Prince of Humanists: author of groundbreaking scholarship and incisive social criticism. Oh, and master of the ancient art of fart concealment.

☞ *How to Sit at the Table, 1530,* page 158. ☜

# *How to Attack an Enemy Ship*

~

## 1441

"When there is fighting, then it is good [to use] jars full of soap and to throw them onto the ship, at the enemies. When the jars break, the soap runs out all over the ship, the warriors slip and fall to the ground…Better than a jar full of soap is one full of hog's fat also called grease. If and when you wish to burn your enemy's ship, hurl there a jar of hog's fat. It works two ways: [men] on the ship cannot hold their feet steady; later, if you throw a small sack or tube full of powder, it burns the ship."

Mariano Taccola, *De ingeneis*

This technique will ensure that your naval battle has all the dignity and gravity of Jell-O wrestling.

# *How to Talk about Your Kids*

~

## 1558

"Those who are constantly talking about their children, their wives or their nursemaids, are equally at fault. 'Yesterday my boy made me laugh so much. Listen to this... You have never seen a more lovable son than my Momo...' No-one has so little to do that he has the time to answer or even to listen to such nonsense, and so it irritates everyone."

Giovanni della Casa, *Il Galateo overo de' costumi*

History teaches us many timeless and important lessons. Chief among them: no one wants to hear about Momo.

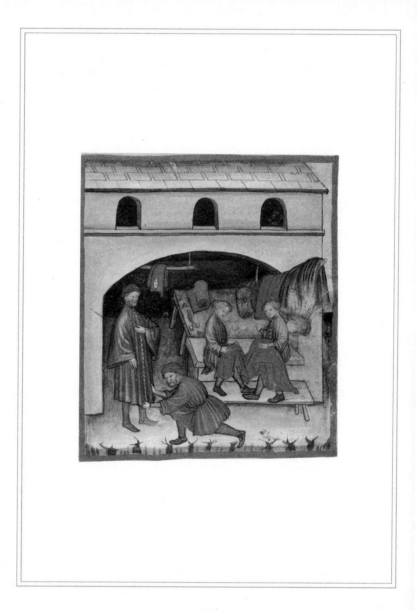

# *How to Look Good on a Budget*

~

## c. 1280

"Your clothing should be pleasing and fine, cut to your figure. If you have no expensive cloth to make clothing, then have it cut nicely from something less than the best, so that it looks good and you appear well dressed. If you lack good clothing, you should accept this: but let your shoes and footwear, belt, purse, and knife be the finest you can have … Be very careful not to wear unkempt clothing, for anything torn is lovelier by far: one appears ill-bred when wearing unkempt clothes, but torn ones simply cannot be helped. It never takes great skill to make something lovely look nice, but one who knows how to wear well what is not lovely appears pleasing and courtly."

Amanieu de Sescás, *Enssenhamen de l'escudier*

The courtly look: it's all in the accessories.

How to Dress to Impress, 1632, page 151.

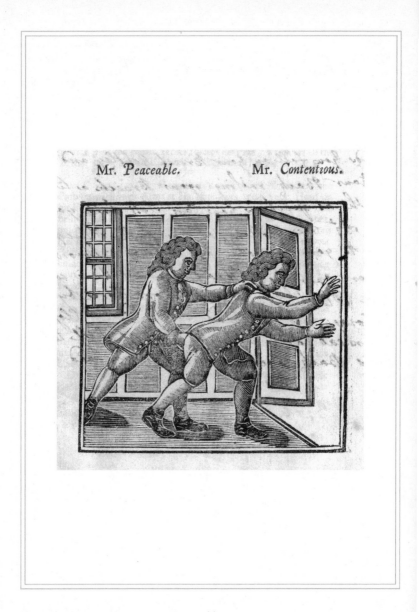
Mr. *Peaceable.*    Mr. *Contentious.*

# How to Get Rid of a Contentious Man

~

1727

"If you have a Companion that disturbs your Mirth, and wou'd be rid of him, with your left Hand take hold of his Collar behind, and with your right put between his Legs as far as his Codpiss, and lift him up easily, and thrust him out of the Room, for he can never turn upon you, but if you lift him too hard, you'll throw him on his nose."

Thomas Parkyns, *Progymnasmata: The inn-play: or, Cornish-hugg wrestler*

Had enough of Mr. Contentious? Just grab him by the codpiece and hurl him away. No wonder they call you Mr. Peaceable.

# *How to Sober Up*

~

## 1612

"That one shall not be drunke. Drink the iuice of Yarrow fasting, and ye shall not be drunke for no drinke, and if you were drunke, it will make you sober, or else eate the marrow of Porke, fasting, and ye shall not be drunke, and if ye be drunke annoint your priuie members in Vinegar, and ye shall waxe sober."

*The Booke of Pretty Conceits*

Bonus: this remedy for drunkenness doubles as a hilarious party trick.

# How to Care for Your Cat

~

## c. 1260

"This animal loves to be lightly stroked by human hands and is playful, especially when it is young. When it sees its own image in a mirror it plays with that and if, perchance, it should see itself from above in the water of a well, it wants to play, falls in, and drowns since it is harmed by being made very wet and dies unless it is dried out quickly. It especially likes warm places and can be kept home more easily if its ears are clipped since it cannot tolerate the night dew dripping into its ears."

Albertus Magnus, *De animalibus*

St. Albert explains cat care.
Cat likes: stroking, mirrors, coziness.
Cat does not like: water, well water, water in ears.

☞ *How to Keep Your Cat*, c. 1470, page 239. 🐟

# How to Trim Your Toenails Underwater

~

## 1789

"To cut the Nails of the Toes in the Water... You must hold your knife in your right hand (if you are right handed) and take up your left leg, and lay the foot on the right knee; there you may take it from the left hand, and with the right cut your Nails without any danger. Thus you may also pick your Toes; and if this way has no other use or advantage yet the dexterity of the management may serve to recommend it."

Melchisédech Thévenot, *The Art of Swimming*

Want to take your backstroke to the next level? Tired of spending valuable exercise time on grooming and vice versa? Here is the lifehack for you.

# How to Walk on Water

~

## 1581

"How to walke on the water. For to doe this, take two little Timbrels, and binde them vnder the soles of thy feete, and at a staues end fasten an other; and with these you maie safely walke on the water, vnto the wonder of all suche as shall see the same: if so be you often exercise the same with a certaine boldnesse and lightnesse of the bodie."

Thomas Hill, *Naturall and Artificiall Conclusions*

Good news: all it takes to walk on water is a couple of tambourines and a quick step. I'm off to practice this unto the wonder of all such as shall be swimming laps at the gym.

# *How to Catch Flies*

~

## c. 1393

"If you have a room or a floor in your dwelling infested with
flies, take little sprigs of fern, tie them together with threads like
tassels, hang them up, and all the flies will settle on them in the
evening. Then take down the tassels and throw them outside...
otherwise, tie a linen stocking to the bottom of a pierced pot and
set the pot in the place where the flies gather and smear the inside
with honey, or apples, or pears. When it is full of flies, place a
platter over the opening, then shake it."

*Le Ménagier de Paris*

Tired of unsightly flypaper? For a more ornamental approach to pest
control, try fern tassels and colander stockings.

☞ *How to Kill Fleas, 1688*, page 69. ☜

# *How to Cure a Nosebleed*

~

## 1673

"Apply to the privy part linnen Cloaths made moist with Vinegar or cold water, blow into the Patients Nostrils a small quantity of the Powder of a Toad prepared, or mix a little of the same with Paste, and apply it to the Pallate with your fingers. If that take no effect, give to the Patient four grains of the Powder thereof in two or three spoonfuls of Plantain water, or in the distilled water of Hogs Dung, for it hath been found effectual where no other Medicine would prevail."

William Sermon, *A Friend to the Sick*

The seventeenth century invites you to play a fun little game called "Nosebleed Remedy or Hazing Ritual?"

# *How to Blow Your Nose*

~

## 1616

"Blowing the nose. We must not blow our nose too lowde, nor open the hand-chercher at all to shewe any nasty filthinesse, nor lay it to the cuppe where another meanes to drinke…"

Thomas Gainsford, *The Rich Cabinet*

Among the genius ideas of the Renaissance: don't smear your snot on someone else's drinking glass. Best practices, folks!

*How to Manage Your Nose, 1640,* page 233.

# *How to Make a Pastry Castle*

~

## c. 1390

"Roll out a leaf of good pastry a foot broad and longer in extent. Make four pastry cases with the roller, each as big around as the smaller part of your arm and six inches deep; put the largest in the middle. Fasten your pastry leaf with its mouth upward, and fasten the other four [to it] at each corner. Carefully carve out crenellations above in the manner of battlements, and dry the pastry hard in an oven or in the sun. In the middle case put a stuffing made of pork with good spices and raw eggs with salt, and colour it with saffron; fill another with almond cream, and keep it white. In another, cow's cream with eggs; colour it red with sanders. In another, stuffing of figs, raisins, apples, and pears; keep it brown. In the other, the filling used for white fritters and colour it with green. Put this in the oven and bake it well, and serve it forth with aquavite."

*The Forme of Cury*

What's better than a nice sturdy castle? A nice sturdy castle filled to the battlements with pork and pudding.

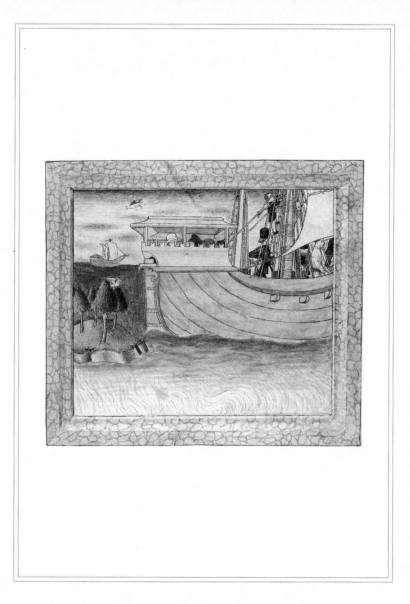

# How to Pack for a Journey

~

## 1480

"[A traveler] should carry with him two bags: one very full of patience, the other containing two hundred Venetian ducats, or at least one hundred and fifty…furthermore, he should provision himself with good Lombard cheese, sausages, tongue, and other cured meats of every sort; white biscuits, some cakes of sugar, and various confections, but not a great quantity because they spoil quickly. Above all he should take plenty of fruit syrup, because that is what keeps a man alive in extreme heat; and also ginger syrup to settle his stomach if it is upset by too much vomiting."

Santo Brasca, *Viaggio in Terrasanta*

Airport security may take your fruit syrups, and customs may confiscate your cured meats, but no one can take away your suitcase full of patience.

# How to Avoid Pregnancy

~

## twelfth century

"If a woman does not wish to conceive, let her carry against her nude flesh the womb of a goat which has never had offspring... In another fashion, take a male weasel and let its testicles be removed and let it be released alive. Let the woman carry these testicles with her in her bosom and let her tie them in goose skin or in another skin, and she will not conceive."

*The Trotula*

Ah, the old goat-womb-against-the-flesh and weasel-balls-in-the-bosom tricks. Yes, those will prevent pregnancy. They will also prevent sex.

☞ *How to Get Pregnant, 1671,* page 211. ☜

# *How to Soothe a Child*

~

## C. 1000

"If a child is very upset, take the same plant [birthwort] and fumigate the child with it. You will make it happier."

*Old English Herbarium*

An upset child is like an angry hive of bees. Fumigate and approach with caution.

# How to Clean Your Teeth

~ .

## 1561

"Take a quarte of water, put an vnce of suger therein, and seth the thirde part of it awaye, strayne it through a cloth, and let it coole, and drinke of it so muche thou listest. It is good also to washe thy mouth in the morninge and at none wyth warme water, and to rubbe thy teth: also to wash the forhead and temples wyth warme water, this clenseth and maketh the head lighte."

Hieronymus Brunschwig, *A Most Excellent and Perfecte Homish Apothecarye*

Next time you run out of mouthwash, try a simple sugar syrup.

How to Whiten Your Teeth, 1686, page 155.

# *How to Cure a Headache*

~

## ninth century

"Headaches you will enchant: take some earth, touch your breast three times and say: My head hurts, why does it hurt? It does not hurt."

Pseudo-Pliny

Good old denial: works better than ibuprofen, every time.

# How to Give Someone Gas

~

## 1660

"A light to make one Fart. The Operation of this Lamp is wonderfull, which so long as a man holds it, he shall not leave Farting untill he let it go: Take the blood of a Snaile and dry it in Linnen Cloath, and make a Candle with it, and light it, and give it to whom he please, and say, be thou lighted: so shall he not leave Farting till he let it go, which is wonderfull."

Johann Jacob Wecker, *Eighteen Books of the Secrets of Art & Nature*

With these candles, your next power outage, birthday party, or romantic dinner will be truly *wonderfull*.

# How to Grow a Beard

~

## 1544

"To make hair and beard grow. Take honeybees in quantity and dry them in a basket by the fire, then make a powder of them, which you moisten with olive oil, and with this ointment, dab several times the place where you would like to have hair, and you will see miracles."

*Traicté nouveau, intitulé, Bastiment de receptes*

Know what's even better than a beard? A beard made of *bees*.
Ladies will go wild.

## *How to Breed Horses*

~

### 1620

"About 8. or 10. dayes, before the Horse and Mare come to the action, being both of them in great lust and courage, feede them for euerie of those daies, with such sweete oates and old dry sweet wheat, equall in mixture and quantitie…and for the better & fuller accomplishment of the action, for those viii. or ten daies, put into euerie gallon of the water they drink (if they be of value and estimation) a pinte of white Wine…and sometime giue betwixt them a pottle of strong stale Beere or Ale, with a greate toste of wheate breade, and let the Stable be kept moste cleane and sweet."

Nicholas Morgan, *The Horse-Mans Honour*

This regimen would get anyone ready for action: delicious dinner, comfortable quarters, and some booze. Oh, and a nice big piece of toast.

# How to Dress Your Child

~

## C. 1200

"Only cheap clothes should be given to little children. They smudge them with ashes, they stain them, they drool on them with their mouths, they wipe noses dripping with slime on their sleeves."

Daniel of Beccles, *Urbanus magnus*

Practical parenting advice from the Middle Ages: just throw an old sack on the child until it stops dripping.

☞ *How to Feed Your Child, 1692,* page 187. ☜

# How to Care for Your Lute

~

## 1676

"And that you may know how to shelter your Lute, in the worst
of Ill weathers, (which is moist) you shall do well, ever when you
Lay it by in the day-time, to put It into a Bed, that is constantly
used, between the Rug and Blanket; but never between the Sheets,
because they may be moist with Sweat, &c…Therefore, a Bed
will secure from all These Inconveniences, and keep your Glew so
Hard as Glass, and All safe and sure; only to be excepted, That
no Person be so inconsiderate, as to Tumble down upon the Bed
whilst the Lute is There; For I have known several Good Lutes
spoil'd with such a Trick."

Thomas Mace, *Musick's Monument*

Think of your lute as a puppy: all it wants is to snuggle in your bed.
*Please?*

# How to Dress for Dancing

~

1538

"You must always be garbed to perfection and your codpiece must be well tied. We sometimes see codpieces slip to the ground during the basse dance so you must tie them well."

Antonius Arena, *Leges dansandi*

Oh, *that* anxiety dream: you're getting your basse dance on with a shapely demoiselle when suddenly you realize that the codpiece on the floor is yours. Don't be that guy!

# How to Slim Down in Fourteen Days

~

## 1579

"An excellent and approued thing to make them slender, that are grosse. Let them eate three or foure cloues of Garlick, with as much of Bread and butter euery morning and euening, first and last, neyther eating nor drinking of three or fowre howers after their taking of it in the morning for the space of fouretene dayes at the least: and drinke euery daye three good draftes of the decoction of Fennel, that is: of the water wherein Fennell is sodde, and well streyned, fowretene daies after at the least, at morning, noone and night. I knewe a man that was maruelous grosse, and could not go a quarter of a myle, but was enforst to rest him a doosen tymes at the least: that with this medicine tooke away his grosnes, and after coulde iourney verye well on foote."

Thomas Lupton, *A Thousand Notable Things*

The Garlic Bread Cleanse: pure genius. After fourteen days of this regimen you'll be rid of that pesky grossenesse and ready to hit the beach. On foote.

# *How to Fatten Up*

~

## 1665

"To make the body or any part thereof plump and fat, that was before too leane…Let your chamber in the summer time be kept something cool and moist with violets, lillies, or the like fresh flowers…When you eate take nothing that is salt or sharp, bitter or too hot, but let your meats be sweet and of good nourishment, as fresh egs, mutton, veale, capon, and for three hours after meat take your recreation in dauncing, singing, discoursing &c. use some baths twice a month…Take twelve or thirteen Lizards or [n]euts cut off their heads and tails, boile them and let the water stand to cool, take of the grease mix it with wheaten flower, feed a Hen therewith till shee be fat, then kil her and eat her; this often used will make you exceeding fat, keep it for a rare and true secret."

Thomas Jeamson, *Artificiall Embellishments*

Mutton, dancing, and the twice-monthly bath are well and good, but never reveal the newty secret of your perfect plumpness.

# How to Prevent Back Pain

~

## c. 1470

"If you avoid wiping your rear end with grass or any other foliage which has grown in the earth, you will never suffer from back pain."

*Les Evangiles des Quenouilles*

You may think your clever foliage regimen is saving money on toilet paper, but take it from the fifteenth century: *it's not worth it.*

# How to Ride a Horse

~

## C. 1260

"And if you go by horse, watch out for false steps; and if you go in the city, I remind you to go very courteously. Ride nicely, with your head a little downcast, rather than riding rampant with vulgarity; and don't look at the heights of each house that you find; watch out that you don't move like a man from the country; don't slide like an eel, but go steadily on the way and among the people."

Brunetto Latini, *Il Tesoretto*

Not everyone is cut out for city driving: either keep your rampant vulgarity in check, or slither back where you came from.

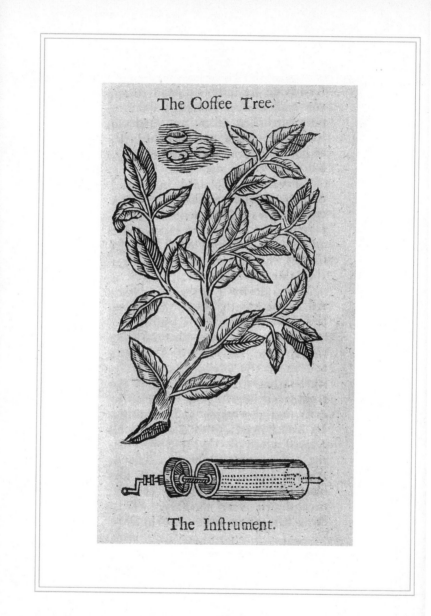

The Coffee Tree.

The Instrument.

48

# How to Make Coffee

~

## 1685

"We must now particularize the preparation of this Drink made with Coffee…The Grain…is put into an Iron Instrument firmly shut together with the coverlid; through this Instrument they thrust a Spit, by the means whereof they turn it before the Fire, till it shall be well rosted; after which having beaten it into very fine Powder, you may make use thereof…and put it into a glass of boyling Water, putting a little Sugar thereto: And after having let it boyl a small time, you must pour it into little dishes of porcelain or any other sort, and so let it be drunk by little and little, as hot as it can possibly be indur'd."

Philippe Sylvestre Dufour, *The Manner of Making Coffee,*
*Tea and Chocolate*

The barista will be delighted to oblige, I'm sure. For clarity, bring along a diagram of The Instrument.

# How to Eat Soup

~

## 1595

"And beware thou soupe not thy pottage, but eate it leisurely with a spoone, without taking it into thy mouth greedily, forcibly drawing thy breath with it, as some clownes do vse, sounding at the receipt of euery spoonefull *Slurrop*. Beware also that thou spill no pottage nor sauce, either on the tablecloth, or on thy clothes."

William Fiston, *The Schoole of Good Manners*

OK, clown, here are the Dos and Don'ts of pottage:
do use your spoon; don't slurrop.

# How to Cure Seasickness

~

## 1695

"Others assure me, That the best Remedy is, to keep always, night and day, a piece of Earth under the Nose; for which purpose they provide a sufficient quantity of Earth, and preserve it fresh in a Pot of Clay; and when they have us'd a piece so long till it begins to grow dry, they put it in again into the Pot, and take out some fresh Earth."

Maximilien Misson, *A New Voyage to Italy*

In addition to abating seasickness, the earth treatment will also create the illusion of a handsome mustache. Win!

# How to Give Birth

~

## c. 1450

"I advise you to scream loudly, so that everyone will believe that you are in great pain, and your husband and the other members of the household will have compassion, and they will try to put out the great fire of your pain by serving you capons, candied almonds, and fine wines."

Michele Savonarola, *Ad mulieres ferrarienses*

Don't worry about labor. But do make sure you play your cards right, because there just might be some fine wines in it for you.

 *How to Care for a Newborn, 1256,* page 214.

# How to Have a Performing Dog

~

## c. 1260

"The dog is by far the most easily taught animal. They therefore learn the mimetic works of actors. If anyone should wish to find this out for himself, let him take a dog born out of a vixen or from a fox, if that can be done. If it cannot, let him take a red dog from among those that are his watchdogs and let him accustom it while it is young to keeping the company of a monkey. For with her he becomes accustomed to do many human things. And if he should have intercourse with the monkey and the monkey should give birth to a dog, that dog will be the most praiseworthy of all for games."

Albertus Magnus, *De animalibus*

Oh, come on. Can *you* think of anything more entertaining than a performing monkey-dog?

☞ *How to Care for Your Dog, c. 1393,* page 205. ☜

# *How to Fold Fabulous Napkins*

~

## 1629

"You make a herringbone pattern out of the napkins…From the herringbone pattern you can make all of the main animals…a castle with its sentinels and artillery pieces, and a fully equipped ship…pyramids, large birds like ostriches, peacocks, storks, human pyramids, centaurs, and other ingenious and charming inventions, for instance an entire hunt on your table made out of napkins."

*Li tre trattati di messer Mattia Giegher*

And after your marvelous napkin castle is complete, you must be prepared to die defending it from guests wanting to wipe their mouths.

# How to Cure Laryngitis

~

## 1579

"Laye a thynne peece of rawe Beefe, to the forehead of them that haue lost theyr voyce, and let it lye thereto all nyght vnremoued: and it wyll helpe them presently, or at the least within three or fowre seuerall applications."

Thomas Lupton, *A Thousand Notable Things*

After three or four applications the patient will not only be speaking, but also screaming at you to stop plastering him with raw beef.

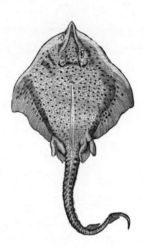

# How to Catch a Ray

~

1658

"When the Fisherman sees the Pastinaca, or Ray, swimming, he leaps ridiculously in his Boat, and begins to play on the Pipe; the Pastinaca is much taken with it, and so comes to the top of the water, and another lays hold of him."

Giambattista della Porta,
*Natural Magick, in XX Bookes*

File under "Closely Guarded Secrets of Rugged Outdoorsmen."

# How to Raise Your Child

~

## twelfth century

"There should be different kinds of pictures, cloths of diverse colors, and pearls placed in front of the child, and one should use nursery songs and simple words; neither rough nor harsh words (such as those of Lombards) should be used in singing in front of the child. After the hour of speech has approached, let the child's nurse anoint its tongue frequently with honey and butter, and this ought to be done especially when speech is delayed. One ought to talk in the child's presence frequently and easy words ought to be said."

*The Trotula*

Yes, pearls are a choking hazard. But let's be serious: the real threat to your child's well-being is the harsh songs of the Lombards.

☞ *How to Dress Your Child, c. 1200*, page 37. 🖎

# *How to Interpret Dreams*

~

## C. 1100

- Being embraced by a man you love: this is useful.
- A dream of hot waters bubbling up: this is bad.
- Falling from a horse: consider this to be great disaster.
- If you are sitting in feces, you will experience all manner of harm.
- Beautifying your head is a good sign.
- Embracing your mother is a very good dream.
- Vomiting in one's dream causes loss, my friend.
- Eating hard-shelled seafood signifies illness.
- Wine of the best vintage: expect joy.

*Oneirocriticon of Germanus*, excerpts

Sitting in feces is unlucky in waking life, too, my friend.

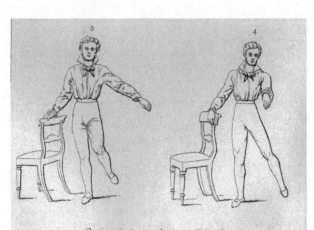

Swimming — Action of the Feet.

# How to Swim Like a Man

~

## 1860

"Every swimmer should use short drawers, and might, in particular places, use canvass slippers. It is even of great importance to be able to swim in jacket and trousers."

Donald Walker, *Walker's Manly Exercises*

You have to get to a job interview, and the bridge is out. Do you miss the appointment, or arrive in your short drawers? Neither. You wear your suit. Like a man.

☛ *How to Trim Your Toenails Underwater, 1789,* page 20. ☚

# How to Cook a Porcupine

~

## 1570

"Get a porcupine in August because at that time, owing to its feeding, it is very fat, even though its flesh has a less bad odour between October and January. After the animal has been killed let the flesh hang, in winter for four days and in summer for a day and a half. When it is skinned, divide it crosswise...stud it with some cloves of garlic and whole cloves and rosemary tips to take away its bad smell. Then set it to roast on a spit, catching the drippings. When it is done serve it up hot, dressed with a garnish of must syrup, rose vinegar, pepper, cinnamon, cloves and the drippings."

Bartolomeo Scappi, *Opera*

And then just discard the whole stinking mess and order takeout.

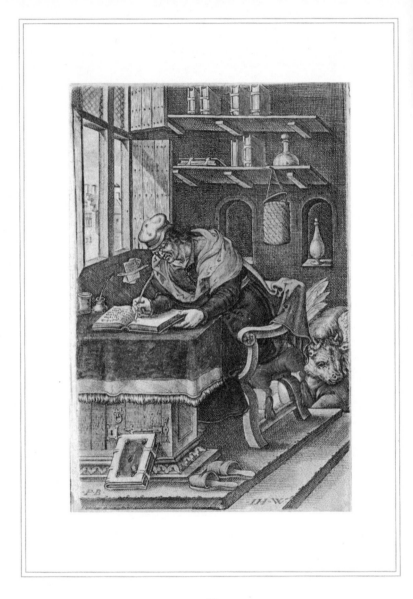

# *How to Party Like a Scholar*

~

## 1558

"It is not appropriate to be always depressed or distracted in the company of others. This may be acceptable to those who have long pursued studies that are called, so I have been told, liberal or intellectual. It should not under any circumstance be permitted among ordinary people."

Giovanni della Casa, *Il Galateo overo de' costumi*

They're called liberal arts because they liberate you from the duty to socialize without weeping.

# How to Make a Dragon out of Fireworks

~

## 1658

"The body of the Dragon must be made either with Past-board, or with fine rods of wicker, being hollow, with a place in the belly to put in two Rockets…first set it at the eyes and mouth…then fire that Rocket which is placed with his mouth toward the tayl of the Dragon, which will make it seem to cast fire from thence till he come to the end of his motion; and then on a sudden (as a creature wounded with some accident) shall return with fire coming forth of his belly: This being well ordered, will give good content to the beholders of the same."

John White, *A Rich Cabinet*

If this spectacle goes according to plan, the "dragon" will hurtle around spewing fire. If it goes awry, the fireworks technician will do the same. Either way, the beholders will be amazed.

# How to Garden with Lobsters

~

1777

"Procure the hollow claws of Lobsters, Crabs, &c. and hanging them in different parts of the garden, the insects creep into them, and are easily taken; but the claws must be often searched."

*The Complete Vermin-Killer*

The problem with this technique is that you'll have to eat a lot of lobsters. Organic gardening is full of hardships.

109. Excercise.

ENCICLOPEDIA

# *How to Exercise*

~

## 1623

"[W]hen the skinne shall be wet with sweat, it shall be good to desist from exercise, lest by proceeding therein, not onely the spirits and good humours be exhausted, but also the fat…bee melted, or at least caused to putrifie; by meanes whereof, if sudden death ensue not, as oftentimes it doth…the body become sickly, withered, and impatient of cold…the best and most profitable exercises, for them that are sound and healthfull, are walking, bowling, the racket, and such like easie exercises."

Tobias Venner, *Via recta ad vitam longam*

For the love of God, don't use the elliptical machine.
Does putrefied fat *sound* like a joke?

# How to Wash Your Hair

~

## twelfth century

"After leaving the bath, let her adorn her hair, and first of all let her wash it with a cleanser such as this. Take ashes of burnt vine, the chaff of barley nodes, and licorice wood (so that it may the more brightly shine), and sowbread…with this cleanser let the woman wash her head. After the washing, let her leave it to dry by itself, and her hair will be golden and shimmering…If the woman wishes to have long and black hair, take a green lizard and, having removed its head and tail, cook it in common oil. Anoint the head with this oil. It makes the hair long and black."

*The Trotula*

Lather. Rinse. Never repeat.

How to Prepare a Bath, c. 1450, page 131.

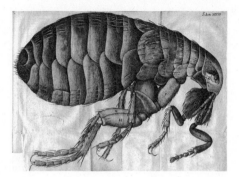

# How to Kill Fleas

~

## 1688

"Take an Earthen Platter, that is broad and shallow, fill it half full with Goats Blood, and set the Platter under the Bed, and all the Fleas will come into it like a swarm of Bees. Or take the Blood of a Bear or Badger, and put it under the Bed, as before, and it gathers the Fleas to it, and they die immediately."

*A Necessary Family-Book*

Just keep in mind that if you are planning a night of passion, you should probably move your miraculous flea-killing apparatus beforehand. A platter of bear's blood under the bed can be kind of a turnoff for some people.

*How to Kill Bedbugs, 1777,* page 2.

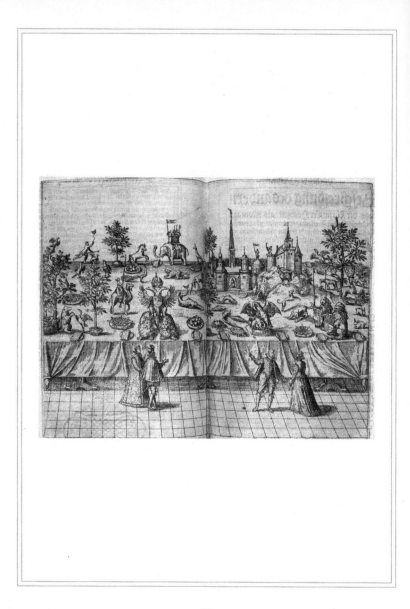

# How to Decorate the Table

~

"One must set a table according to the time of year: in winter, in enclosed and warm places; in summer, in cool and open places. In spring, flowers are arranged in the dining room and on the table; in winter, the air should be redolent with perfumes; in summer, the floor should be strewn with fragrant boughs of trees, of vine, and of willow, which freshen the dining room; in autumn, let the ripe grapes, pears and apples hang from the ceiling. Napkins should be white and the tablecloths spotless, because, if they were otherwise, they would arouse squeamishness and take away the desire to eat."

Bartolomeo Platina, *De honesta voluptate et valetudine*

Flower arrangements are nice, but a heap of downed
tree limbs can really make your dining room reflect the season.
Hurricane season, that is.

# *How to Tell Time*

~

## 1658

"Another excellent Rule, to know the houre of the Day or Night at any time. If any two (or more) Parties be in company together, let one of them take something from the ground, (what they please) and give it to another Party standing by. Now, if the thing taken up hath growne, and may grow againe, as Seeds, Hearbs, or the like, it is then 1. 4. 7. or 10. of the Clock, or very neare. If it did never grow, nor never shall, as Stones, metals, Pot‹sheards, Glasse, or the like, it is then 2. 5. 8. or 11. of the Clocke, or very neare. But if it hath growne, and will never grow again, as Sticks, Chips, Shels, or such like, it is then 3. 6. 9. or 12. of the clocke, or very neare. But remember this Caution. That both they that give the judgement, and they that taketh up the thing, doth not know what houre it is before they try the Conceit."

John White, *A Rich Cabinet*

This technique is guaranteed to be accurate to within an hour or two, provided that you don't check the time either before *or* after you try the Conceit.

# How to Harvest the Mandrake

~

## twelfth century

"It shines at night like a lamp, and when you see it mark it round
quickly with iron lest it escape you. For so strong is this power in
it, that if it sees an unclean man coming to it, it runs away. So for
this reason mark it round with iron and dig about it, taking care
that you do not touch it with the iron; but remove the earth from
it with the utmost care with an ivory stake, and when you have
seen the foot of the plant and its hands, then you shall at once
bind the plant with a new rope, and you shall tie the same round
the neck of a hungry dog, and in front of it place food at a little
distance, so that in its eagerness to get the food it may pull out
the plant."

*Apuleii liber de medicaminibus herbarum*

I'm not sure mandrake farming is worth it, in the end. All that trouble
just because you can't find a clean man to dig up the mandrakes?

# How to Cure Insomnia

~

## 1597

"Pluck up Lettuce with thy left hand before the sun rising, and lay it vnder the couering of a sicke mans bedde, (hee not knowing thereof) to cause him to sleepe; or gather fiue, three, or one of the leaues next the stalke, and lay them vnder his feete, and as many next to the toppe vnder his boulster, hee not knowing of it, to cause him to sleepe."

William Langham, *The Garden of Health*

The patient will be so happy to get some sleep! And so perplexed to discover that he has been sharing his bed with a salad.

# How to Defend Yourself from Basil

~

## 1579

"An Italian, through the ofte smelling of an herbe called Basyll, had a Scorpion bred in his braine; which dyd not onely a long tyme grieue him, but also at the last kylled him... Take heede therefore ye smellers of Basyll."

Thomas Lupton, *A Thousand Notable Things*

Is your pesto obsession really worth the risk of *death by grievous brain scorpion*?

# How to Train Your Cat to Do Tricks

~

## 1809

"Cats may be taught to pull a bell-rope, to fire a pistol and a multitude of similar tricks...A bit of cloth may be attached to the string communicating with the bell, to afford the cat something convenient to seize hold of. It will be easy to induce her to seize it by holding it near her, or by aggravating her a little with it. When she does so, and causes the bell to ring, reward her...Firing off a pistol may follow this, taught in the same way, a piece of cloth being attached to the trigger, and the pistol being secured in a stationary position. Merely snapping the trigger will do at first, then caps may be used, and finally powder."

*Haney's Art of Training Animals*

Aggravated cats and early handguns—what could possibly go wrong?

# How to Make Dinner Conversation

~

## 1576

"The first thing which we ought to obserue at the table is to weigh the estimation and callinge of every geast, and the next to take occasion when he seeth it offred to…minister…profitable and delightsome Questions…First therefore and foremost, this may bee demaunded:

- Whether that the Aier or Meate bee more necessary for the preservation of the life of Manne?
- Why doth the self same drinke seeme stronger to one that is fasting, then to one that is full?
- To begin with the sower belching, it may be demaunded whereof it cometh?
- Is grosse meat good for such as recouer out of sicknes?
- [If] it be good once in a month to be drunken with wine?
- Why doth Wyne which is vnmingled with water sooner cause a mans head to ake then that which is mingled?
- Why do not children which are hoat of complexion, loue wine, which aged persons...do greedely desire?
- Doth Wine hurt the brayne?
- Whether Fishes do feed vpon their owne frie or not?
- Do Fishes chawe their meat?
- Beanes beeing windy, why do they not lose that euill quality by boyling, as well as barly?"

Thomas Twyne, *The Schoolemaster, or Teacher of Table Philosophie*, excerpts

Nothing makes for delightsome dinner conversation like an endless barrage of questions about drink, digestion, and flatulence. Doth wine hurt the brayne? Who knows, but these questions sure do.

# *How to Treat Baldness*

~

## thirteenth century

"By frequently rubbing your bald spots with ground onions, you will be able to recover the charm of your head."

*Regimen sanitatis Salernitanum*

Even if this remedy fails, an onion-greased scalp
is definitely charming.

# How to Attract a Lover

~

## 1699

"To make an Enchanted Ring, to cause one to fall in love with you. Get a hollow Ring, steep Goats hair taken from the Beard, steep it in the juice of Night Shade, or Wake Robin, an herb so called, pull it through the Ring, and whoever wears it, it shall cause them to fall in love with you."

*Aristotle's Legacy: or, his Golden Cabinet of Secrets Opened*

Years down the road, it will be so sweet to reminisce with your lover about the goat-beard caper that brought you together.

☞ *How to Increase Lust, eleventh century,* page 88. ☜

# *How to Train Your Sparrow Hawk*

~

## c. 1393

"From the moment your sparrow hawk is first placed on the fist, be careful that it not be upset by you or anyone else. Understand, my dear, that anything that happens unexpectedly, suddenly, and tempestuously—whether person, animal, rock, stool, stick, or anything else—disturbs and agitates it strongly…Any time that it holds or grips you, do not upset yourself or it. Rather, detach it gently, without agitating yourself or it, no matter what pain it inflicts on you, for if you vex it one single time, it will never again love you…at this point in the training of the hawk, it is more crucial than before to hold it on the fist and carry it to court and among people, to churches and other assembly places and through the street, and hold it on the fist continuously, day and night, as long as possible."

*Le Ménagier de Paris*

Falconry is a rewarding hobby! Just make sure that you never put the bird down or make a sudden movement, even when its talons tear into your flesh during church, because then it will hate you forever.

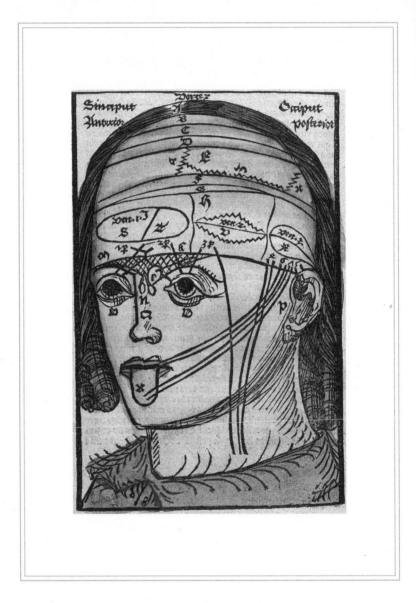

# *How to Clear Your Head*

~

## 1623

"The excrements of the braine must daily bee avoyded through the mouth by spetting, and excreation, through the nose by exsufflation, and also sometimes by sternutation, especially in the mornings; and those of the breast by coughing expectorated. And thus much for excretions."

Tobias Venner, *Via recta ad vitam longam*

Don't forget to work a little coughing and spitting into your morning routine. You do *not* want to start your day with a head full of brain excrement.

# How to Increase Lust

~

## eleventh century

"There are the foods like the ones we spoke about—pepper and octopus, pine-nuts, figs, fresh meat, brains, and eggs yolks. Suitable for potions as well are skink, and "wolf-testicles"—that is, rag-wort—becaue it rouses lust like the skink...Pills for the impotent. Take equal quantities of seed of white onions, rag-wort, the brains of sparrows, flowers of male palm, and white incense. Temper with warm water and shape into pills the size of chick-peas. Give seven in the morning, with wine—and no more, because if you give more, the woman will faint beneath him."

Constantinus Africanus, *Liber de coitu*

Forget Viagra. If you really want to impress your partner, talk to your doctor about whether skink potion is right for you.

# How to Make Your
# Own Lip Balm

~

## 1579

"If one vse to rubbe chapped or rough lyppes, with the sweat behinde their eares, it wyll make them fyne, smothe, and well culloured: a thing proued."

Thomas Lupton, *A Thousand Notable Things*

Just don't apply your balm in public.

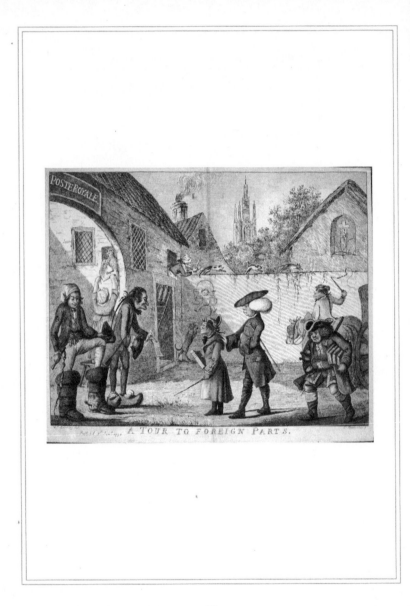

A TOUR TO FOREIGN PARTS.

# *How to Interview People Abroad*

~

## 1789

"A traveller's memory will be greatly relieved, by putting down the queries he wishes to have answered...

- Is it easy for ships of war to land on the sea coast, or is landing rendered hazardous by sands? and rocks?
- Which are the favourite herbs of the sheep of this country?
- How far are the merchants of this country secured against the pyratical powers of Barbary?
- What is the general value of whales of different sizes?
- What celebrated ladies are still living, and worth to be taken notice of for their extraordinary qualifications?"

Leopold Berchtold, *An Essay to Direct and Extend the Inquiries of Patriotic Travellers*, excerpts

Careful with your questions there, traveler. The locals will assume you're plotting to raid their coasts, beguile their sheep, sell their whales of different sizes, and take notice of their celebrated ladies.

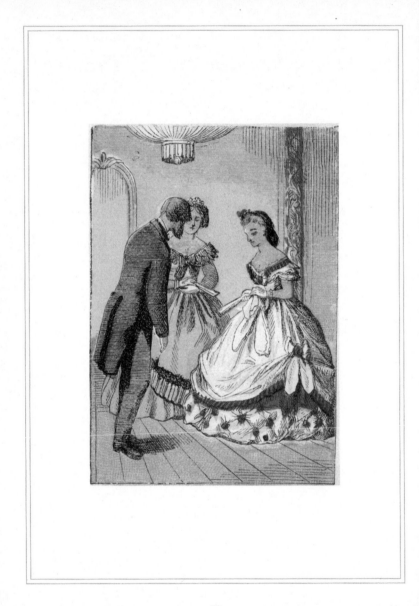

# How to Avoid an Acquaintance

~

## 1881

"If a person desires to avoid a bowing acquaintance with a person who has been properly introduced, he may do so by looking aside, or dropping the eyes as the person approaches, for, if the eyes meet, there is no alternative, bow he must."

John H. Young, *Our Deportment*

A smooth, time-honored technique for avoiding What's-her-face you met at that party: look at your shoes.

# How to Make a Tattoo

~

## 1563

"For to write letters vpon a mans body or face that shall neuer be rubbed out. You muste goe into the stooues or hoate houses whych be verie hote, and when you are in a sweate wryte vpon your bodye wyth what Inke you wil, then cut the skynne wyth a sharpe rasour, and fill the cuttes wyth earthe of what coloure you wyll, and leaue theym so and incontinent by reason of the great heate the skynne wyll close and shut up togyther and the letters or fygures that you haue made vpon youre fleshe will remaine for euer."

Alessio Piemontese, *The Second Part of the Secretes of Maister Alexis of Piemont*

The secret tools of DIY Body Art: a sauna and some dirt.

# How to Make Bird Missiles

~

## thirteenth century

"Another kind of fire for burning enemies wherever they are. Take petroleum, black petroleum, liquid pitch, and oil of sulphur. Put all these in a pottery jar buried in horse manure for fifteen days. Take it out and smear with it crows which can be flown against the tents of the enemy. When the sun rises and before the heat has melted it the mixture will inflame. But we advise that it should be used before sunrise or after sunset."

Marcus Graecus, *Liber ignium ad comburendos hostes*

Revealed: the origins and operational tactics of Angry Birds.

TRANSPLANTING OF TEETH.

# How to Cure a Toothache

~

## 1779

"The tooth-ach is often occasioned by an impure serum, which corrodes the membranes and nerves; very frequently brought on by colds, and rheumatic complaints, more particularly after a sudden change of weather…The best radical cure is to extract the tooth, if it can be conveniently effected. If the tooth affected be not one of the grinders, it may be replaced by one drawn fresh from a healthy person, which often becomes as useful and lasting as the original one could have been."

*The London Practice of Physic*

Jealous of your friend's perfect smile? It can be yours! No, really—just take it and put it in your mouth.

# How to Have a Beautiful Child

~

## 1697

"In case of Similitude, nothing is more powerful than the Imagination of the Mother, for if she fasten her Eyes upon any Object, and imprint it in her Mind, it oft times so happens, that the Child in some part or other of its Body has a representation thereof…Many Women big with Child, seeing a Hare cross them, will through the strength of Imagination bring forth a Child with a hairy Lip. Some Children are born with flat Noses, wry Mouths, great blubber Lips, and ill-shap'd Bodies; and most ascribe the reason to the Imagination of the Mother, who has cast her Eyes and Mind upon some ill-shap'd and distorted Creatures: Therefore it behoves all Women with Child to avoid such sights, if possible; or at least, not to regard 'em."

*Aristotle's Master-piece Compleated*

Sorry, expectant mothers. No wine, no sushi, no soft cheeses. And now you can forget about the zoo, the aquarium, and the circus, too.

☞ *How to Give Birth, c. 1450*, page 52. 🖐

# How to Mix Drinks for Ladies

~

1892

"The Ladies' Great Favorite. A large glass, a squirt of Seltzer, a spoonful of fine sugar, fill a wineglass half full with sherry and the other half with port wine, 1 dash of brandy; mix this well. Fill your glass with shaved ice; ornament with orange and pineapple, and top it off with ice-cream; serve with a spoon."

William Schmidt, *The Flowing Bowl*

A true girly drink includes a fruit salad, a sundae, *and* a snow cone.

# *How to Relieve Yourself*

~

## C. 1200

"If it is necessary to empty one's bowels in a wood or field, the one relieving himself should face into the wind, and squat in the shadows while he is at it. When he is done, he should wipe with his left hand. While your enemy is emptying his bowels, do not seek revenge against him; it is detestable to harm someone while he is squatting…Do not let your arse emit silent farts under your leg; it is disgraceful when others notice a person's stench. If a storm is brewing in your bowels, find a place where you can empty them."

Daniel of Beccles, *Urbanus magnus*

Ah, look: a perfect little pile of wisdom from a shadowy corner of the Middle Ages.

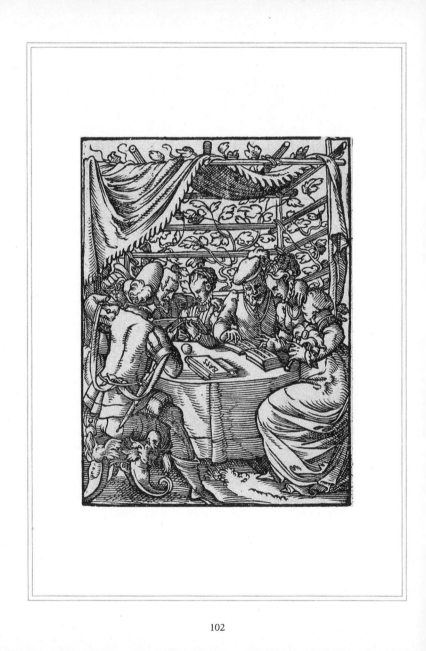

# *How to Sing*

~

## 1650

"A singer should not sing through his nose. He must not stammer, lest he be incomprehensible. He must not push with his tongue or lisp, else one will hardly understand half of what he says. He also should not close his teeth together, nor open his mouth too wide, nor stretch his tongue out over his lips, nor thrust his lips upward, nor distort his mouth, nor disfigure his cheeks and nose like the long-tailed monkey, nor crumple his eyebrows together, nor wrinkle his forehead, nor roll his head or the eyes therein round and round, nor wink with the same, nor tremble with his lips, etc."

Christoph Bernhard, *Von der Singe-Kunst oder Manier*

Don't let your singing career be ruined by the age-old problem of Bitchy Singing Face.

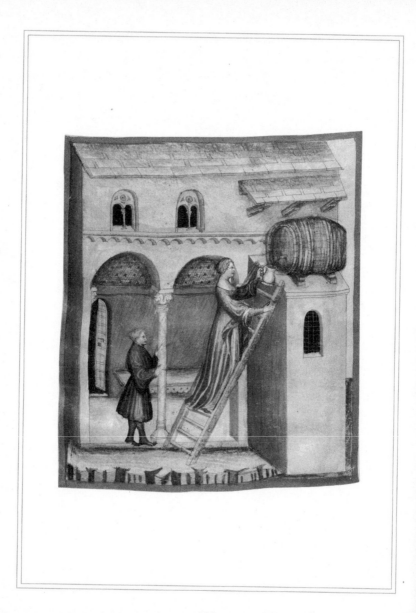

# *How to Serve Wine to Your Toddler*

~

## C. 1450

"I will speak briefly about care of the child up to the age of seven…concerning wine, children should always drink common wine, diluted more or less according to the strength of the wine and the lesser or greater age of the child, because older children can drink their wine mixed with less water; white is better than red."

Michele Savonarola, *Ad mulieres ferrarienses*

The author does not explain what type of wine pairs best with mashed bananas.

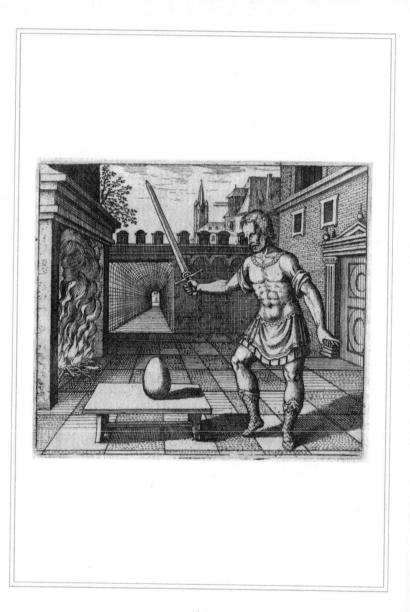

# *How to Make a Giant Egg*

~

## 1660

"To make a great compound Egg as big as twenty Eggs. Take twenty eggs, part the whites from the yolks and strain the whites by themselves, and the yolks by themselves; then have two bladders, boil the yolks in one bladder, fast bound up as round as a ball, being boild hard put it in another bladder, and the whites round about it, binde it up round like the former, and being boild it will be a perfect egg. This serves for grand sallets. Or you may adde to these yolks of eggs, musk and ambergreece, candied pistaches, grated bisket bread, and sugar, and to the whites almond paste, musk, juyce of oranges, and beaten ginger, and serve it with butter, almond milk, sugar, and juyce of oranges."

Robert May, *The Accomplisht Cook*

So those are your options. Make a giant egg, and serve it with a giant salad. Or raid your pantry for ingredients to make a giant, musky, pistachio-pocked, orange-juice egg, and serve it with queasy regret. *Bon appétit!*

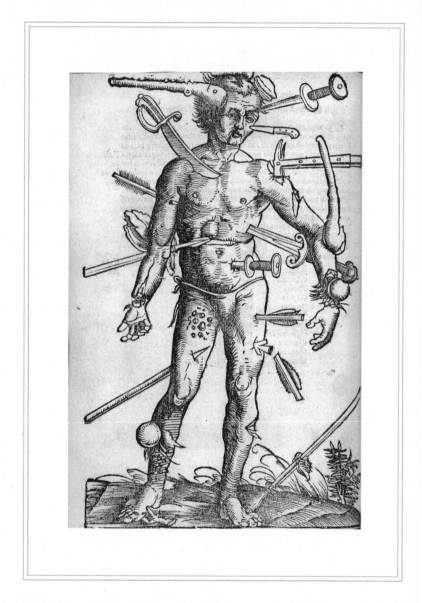

# How to Heal All Wounds

~

## 1686

"A Drink that healeth all Wounds... Take Sanicle, Milfoil, and Bugle, of each a like quantity, stamp them in a Mortar, and temper them with Wine, and give the sick that is wounded to drink twice or thrice a day till he be whole: Bugle holdeth open the wound, Milfoil cleanseth the wound, Sanicle healeth it; but Sanicle may not be given to him that is hurt in the Head, or in the Brain-pan, for it is dangerous. This is a good and tryed Medicine."

Hannah Woolley, *The Accomplish'd Ladies Delight*

Sanicle, Milfoil, and Bugle: sounds like a law firm, but no! It turns out they are a highly regarded team of paramedic elves specializing in trauma care.

# How to Care for Your Lawn

~

## c. 1260

"Nothing refreshes the sight so much as fine short grass. One must clear the space destined for a pleasure garden of all roots, and this can hardly be achieved unless the roots are dug out, the surface is levelled as much as possible, and boiling water is poured over the surface, so that the remaining roots and seeds which lie in the ground are destroyed and cannot germinate ... The ground must then be covered with turves cut from good [meadow] grass, and beaten down with wooden mallets, and stamped down well with the feet until they are hardly able to be seen. Then little by little the grass pushes through like fine hair, and covers the surface like a fine cloth."

Albertus Magnus, *De vegetabilibus*

With the time required for boiling water and malleting turf, yard work may take up your whole weekend. But just think how much your neighbors will envy your fine short grass.

# *How to Dress for Bathing*

~

## 1881

"Flannel is the best material for a bathing costume, and gray is regarded as the most suitable color. It may be trimmed with bright worsted braid. The best form is the loose sacque, or the yoke waist, both of them to be belted in, and falling about midway between the knee and the ankle; an oilskin cap to protect the hair from the water, and merino socks to match the dress, complete the costume."

John H. Young, *Our Deportment*

Sunburn and love handles are no problem when you're in your flannel sack. The only drawback is that other swimmers may mistake you for a walrus.

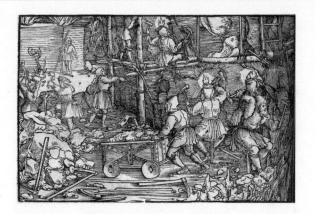

# How to Get Rich

~

## 1556

"Of all ways whereby great wealth is acquired by good and honest means, none is more advantageous than mining... So let the farmers have for themselves the fruitful fields and cultivate the fertile hills for the sake of their produce; but let them leave to miners the gloomy valleys and sterile mountains, that they may draw forth from these, gems and metals which can buy, not only the crops, but all things that are sold."

Georgius Agricola, *De re metallica*

If you really want to get rich, quit your zucchini farming and go find some gems and metals. You may not have considered how many things you can buy with a mine full of gems, but the answer is *all the things*.

# How to Caper in Water

~

## 1595

"To caper with both his legges at once aboue the water. Lying vpon his backe straight as afore, his hands with their palmes downwards, pressing the water the better to keepe him vp, he must cast both his legges out of the water at once, and caper with them vpward as men vse to doe downward in dauncing, as thus."

Everard Digby, *A Short Introduction for to Learne to Swimme*

When you're trying to impress fellow swimmers at the pool, sometimes the backstroke just isn't enough. This aquatic daunce will entrance onlookers with the sight of your legs capering gloriously past in the slow lane.

116

# How to Change a Diaper

~

## 1612

"How the child must be made cleane...The Nurse, or some other, must sit neere the fire, laying out her legges at length, hauing a soft pillow in her lap, the dores and windowes being close shut, and hauing something about her, that may keep the wind from the child...If he be verie foule, shee may wash him with a little water and wine lukewarme, with a spunge or linnen cloth. The time of shifting him is commonly about seuen a clocke in the morning, then againe at noone, and at seuen a clocke at night: and it would not be amisse, to change him againe about midnight; which is not commonly done. But...after he hath slept a good while, do every time shift him; lest he should foule and bepisse himselfe."

Jacques Guillemeau, *Child-birth or, The happy deliverie of women*

The fireside yoga pose and the windproof cape increase the difficulty level a little. On the plus side, you only have to do it three times a day, and wine is involved.

☞ *How to Protect Your Infant, 1697*, page 194. 🐟

Aurantia     Pomrantzen.

# *How to Use an Orange*

~

1722

"[The orange is a] large round Fruit, green at first, and of a reddish yellow Colour, cover'd with a tough Skin or Peel, under which is contain'd the Pulp, consisting of a great Number of small *Vesiculae*, full of a sharp Juice…The Juice of Oranges is used as Sauce to whet the Appetite. It is cordial and cooling, good to quench Thirst, and serviceable in burning Fevers; it is of great Use in the Scurvy."

Joseph Miller, *Botanicum officinale*

There is nothing more cordial than an orange. If only we had a word for its charming reddish-yellow color…

# *How to Kill Snakes*

~

## 1688

"1. How to gather Snakes and Adders to one place. Take one handful of Onion, and ten River Crab-fish, pound them together, and lay it in the places where the Snakes and Adders are, and they will all gather together.

2. To kill Snakes and Adders. Take a large Rhadish, and strike the Adder and Snake with it, and one blow will kill them."

*A Necessary Family-Book*

A simple and elegant technique: lure snakes with a giant crab cake
and then bludgeon them with a radish.

# How to Belch Politely

~

## 1640

"This is also an ill custome, when (by reason of thy full feeding, or couldnesse of stomack, thou hast a provocation to rasp wind) for thee to doe it so carelessely, and with such a noise, that all must take notice of it: but it ought to be done so privately that it may not be perceived, and some are so civill, that when they yawne or raspe winde, they smooth their hand over their faces, as if they were smoothing their beardes, and at the same time, doe cover their mouthes, so that you cannot perceive them."

Lucas Gracián Dantisco, *Galateo espagnol, or The Spanish Gallant*

As if you needed another reason to cultivate a luscious beard: it provides an excellent belch cover.

☞ *How to Grow a Beard, 1544,* page 35. ☜

Titianus pinxit
W. Hollar fecit. 1649.

M.D. XX III &c

RITRATTO DE MONSIG.RE GIO
DELLA CASA.

# How to Tell Jokes

~

## 1558

"Where your pleasantries are not rewarded with the laughter of listeners, cease and desist from telling jokes in the future. The defect is in you, not in your listeners…For these are movements of the mind, and if they are pleasant and lively, they are an indication and a testimonial of the nimble mind and the good habits of the speaker—this is particularly liked by other men and endears us to them. But if they are without grace and charm, they have the contrary effect, so it appears a jackass is joking, or that someone very fat with an enormous butt is dancing and hopping about in a tight-fitting vest."

Giovanni della Casa, *Il Galateo overo de' costumi*

Giovanni della Casa: skilled diplomat, astute social critic, fearsome heckler at Renaissance comedy clubs.

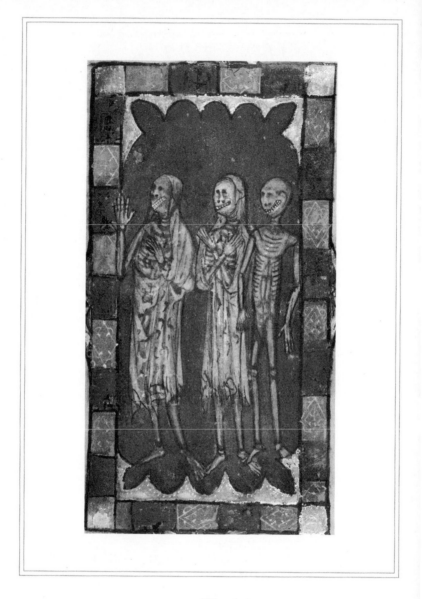

# How to *Make* Someone *Die*
## *of Laughter*

~

## thirteenth century

"Beneath the armpits are certain veins called 'ticklish' which, if
they are cut, cause a man to die of laughter."

Richardus Salernitanus, *Anatomia*

Tired of people not laughing at your jokes? Just stab them
in the armpits.

# How to Make French Toast

~

## 1660

"French Toasts. Cut French Bread, and toast it in pretty thick toasts on a clean gridiron, and serve them steeped in claret, sack, or any wine, with sugar and juyce of orange."

Robert May, *The Accomplisht Cook*

Did you know that "French" is culinary shorthand for "slosh wine all over your breakfast"? With that trick up your sleeve, you'll be mastering the art of French cooking in no time.

# How to Remove a Stain

~

## 1562

"To take all maner of spots out of sylke. Take the iuyce of great and round musheroms of a sharpe taste, weate the spots in it the space of two houres, and than washe them with cleare water, and let them drye."

Alessio Piemontese, *The Thyrde and Laste Parte of the Secretes of the Reverende Maister Alexis of Piemont*

Who needs a stain stick? Just rub a large mushroom on your blouse.

# How to Prepare a Bath

~

## C. 1450

"If your lord wishes to bathe and wash his body clean, hang sheets round the roof, every one full of flowers and sweet green herbs, and have five or six sponges to sit or lean upon, and see that you have one big sponge to sit upon, and a sheet over so that he may bathe there for a while, and have a sponge also for under his feet, if there be any to spare, and always be careful that the door is shut. Have a basin full of hot fresh herbs and wash his body with a soft sponge, rinse him with fair warm rose-water, and throw it over him; then let him go to bed; but see that the bed be sweet and nice; and first put on his socks and slippers that he may go near the fire and stand on his foot-sheet, wipe him dry with a clean cloth, and take him to bed to cure his troubles."

John Russell, *Boke of Nurture*

Does *your* bathing routine involve a bushel of fresh herbage and half a dozen sponges? Hmm, looks like the Middle Ages just schooled you in bathing.

☞ *How to Wash Your Head, 1612,* page 173. 🖎

# How to Be a Head Chef

~

## 1473

"The Cook orders, regulates and is obeyed in his Kitchen; he should have a chair between the buffet and the fireplace to sit on and rest if necessary; the chair should be so placed that he can see and survey everything that is being done in the Kitchen; he should have in his hand a large wooden spoon which has a double function: one, to test pottages and brewets, and the other, to chase the children out of the Kitchen, or to make them work, striking them if necessary."

Olivier de la Marche, *Mémoires*

If you want to be top chef, you have to rule your kitchen with an iron fist and a wooden spoon.

134

# How to Make a Cheesy Omelet

~

## c. 1393

"First, heat the pan thoroughly with oil, butter, or another grease
as you wish, and when it is good and hot all over, especially toward
the handle, mix and pour your eggs into the pan and turn them
often with a spatula, then sprinkle on some good grated cheese.
Know that it needs to be put on top, because if you grind the
cheese with the herbs and eggs, when you fry the omelet, the
cheese on the bottom would stick to the pan. That is what happens
when you mix the eggs with the cheese for an omelet. For this
reason, first put the eggs in the pan, and put the cheese on top,
and then cover with the edge of the eggs; otherwise it will stick to
the pan."

*Le Ménagier de Paris*

If we don't pay attention to the past, we are doomed to repeat its
mistakes. So let's break the cycle and *put the eggs in the pan before
the cheese.*

# How to Cure Pimples

~

## 1665

"To cure Redness and fiery Pimples in the Face…you may spread on the visage the warm blood of a pigeon, pullet, or capon drawn newly from under their wings; let the blood lay on all night, in the morning wash it off with warm water, or the decoction of soap, oatmeal, or the like. Or else in the place of these remedies, Take fresh flesh of a neck of beef, veal, or mutton, cut two or three thin slices, lay them on the red places, and change them often, or else they will stink: And in case you have no fresh flesh, you may take slices of stale, put them on the coals, and so apply them warm to the redness."

Thomas Jeamson, *Artificiall embellishments*

Forget the pharmacy; get straight to the butcher's for your foolproof acne treatments.

# How to Dress for Cycling

~

## 1896

"Modesty is becoming at all times, and especially upon a bicycle...
A prominent physician advises women cyclists to wear woolen
clothing, the head covering light, low shoes, leggings, and no
corsets...The Alpine hat is considered the proper head/gear for
women. Men should wear a short loose/fitting sack coat of some
light woolen material, with knickerbockers to match, woolen
stockings, cap, low shoes and a negligee shirt, or if the day is cold,
a sweater."

John Wesley Hanson, *Etiquette and Bicycling, for 1896*

Cycling attire is simple. Corset, no. Alpine hat, always.

# How to Recover From a Dance Mishap

~

## 1538

"When you fall, pick yourself up quickly, and go back to finishing the dance energetically without complaining at all: *pa-trim pa-tro-lo!*...And if you don't get up, you will not be able to fall any further: there is nowhere to fall for one who is lying on the ground."

Antonius Arena, *Leges dansandi*

If you dance enough, you're bound to end up on your face eventually. You have two options: ponder your existential condition, or pretend it never happened. Pa-trim pa-tro-lo!

# How to Drink Beer

~

## 1623

"Beere that is too bitter of the hop…hurteth the sinewes, offendeth the sight, and causeth the head ach, by filling the ventricles of the braine with troublesome vapors…Here some may demand, Whether it be better to drink their Beere cold, or a little warmed, especially in the Winter season? Whereto I answer, that I see no good reason to approve the drinking thereof warme, as I know some to do, not only in the Winter, but almost all the yeere: for it is nauceous and fulsome to the stomack…Moreover, it doth not so well quench the thirst, temper the naturall heat, and coole the inward parts, as if it be taken cold."

Tobias Venner, *Via recta ad vitam longam*

This just in from the annals of drinking lore: poorly chosen beer gives you brain vapors, and warm beer is nauseating.

# *How to Converse*

~

## 1646

"Neither shake thy head, feet, or legges; Rowle not thine eyes. Lift not one of thine eye-browes higher than thine other. Wry not thy mouth. Take heed that with thy spettle thou bedew not his face with whom thou speakest, and to that end approach not too nigh him."

Francis Hawkins, *Youths Behaviour*

The close-talker: terrorizing conversation partners since the seventeenth century.

# How to Eat Politely

~

## 1646

"If thou soakest thy bread or meat in the sauce, soak it not againe, after that thou hast bitten it, dip therein at each time a reasonable morsell which may be eaten at one mouthfull."

Francis Hawkins, *Youths Behaviour*

From the same authority who told you not to be a close-talker, more timeless advice: don't be a double-dipper.

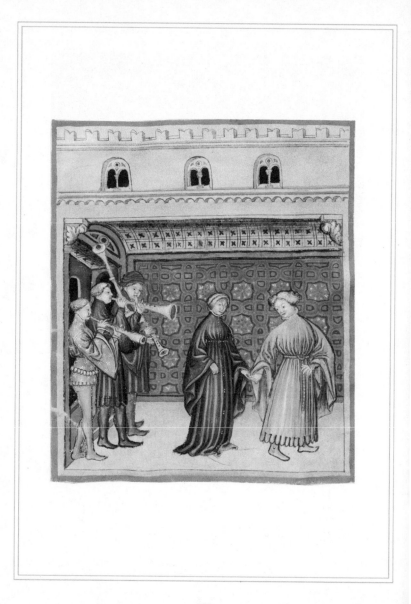

144

# How to Dance

~

## C. 1455

"It is necessary to have a refined agility and physical style. Note that this agility and style under no circumstances should be taken to extremes. Rather, maintain the mean of your movement, that is—not too much nor too little. With smoothness, appear like a gondola that is propelled by two oars through waves when the sea is calm as it normally is. The said waves rise with slowness and fall with quickness...avoid the extremes of the foreigner from the countryside and of him who is a traveling entertainer."

Domenico da Piacenza, *De arte saltandi*

Dance like nobody's watching... and you're a gondola.

☞ *How to Dress for Dancing, 1538,* page 41. ☜

# How to Get Rid of Mosquitoes

~

## c. 1260

"If a house or some other place where there are mosquitos is
fumigated with elephant dung, they are put to flight and die."

Albertus Magnus, *De animalibus*

Yet another reason to keep an elephant on hand.

☞ *How to Catch Flies, c. 1393,* page 23. ☜

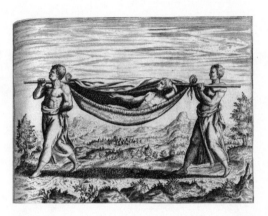

# *How to Sleep While Traveling*

~

## 1700

"I have forgot hitherto to tell you that there is some Incommoditie for Travellers upon the Road, as to their Bedding, their Cloaths especially, the Sheets being for the most part very nasty, and it is but now and then that either money or fair words can procure a Pair of clean Sheets. The best remedy I know is not to put off ones Cloaths, and to wrap ones self, especially the Head, in their Cloak, that the face and Hands may not touch any unclean thing; in short a little Patience will do it, and you will be sure to be better accomodated in good Towns."

Andrew Balfour, *Letters*

This ingenious self-swaddle will defend you from very nasty sheets the world over. *Bon voyage!*

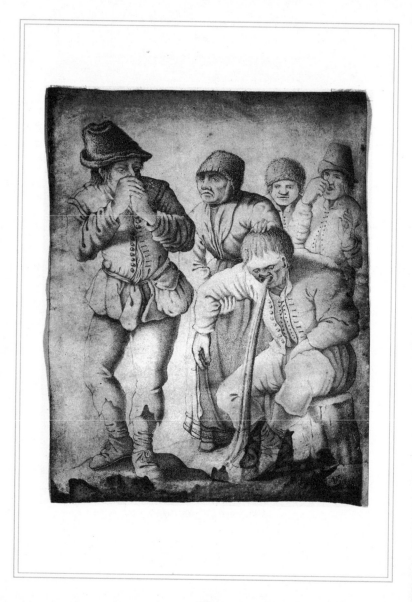

# How to Cure Nausea

~

## 1693

"A speedy Remedy for Fits of Vomiting. Take a large Nutmeg, grate off one half of it, and toast the flat side of the other, till the Oily part begin to ouze or sweat out, then clap it to the Pit of the Patient's Stomach as hot as he can well endure it, and let him keep it on whilst it continues warm, and then if need be put on another."

Robert Boyle, *Medicinal Experiments*

If you're lucky, the patient will be so surprised by the sizzling nutmeg on his abdomen that he will forget all about his nausea.

# *How to Dress to Impress*

~

"So as a man bee neatly attired, it doth not import to bee gorgious. It is sufficient if he haue alwayes clean linnen and white, that he be well shod: as for his apparell, if it be not rich, yet, at the least it must not bee old nor filthy, let his hat be new, and of the newest fashion; let him alwayes haue his head dried, and his hayre in order as they wear them; let him keep his beard carefully in order, by reason of the discommodity he shold otherwise receiue in speaking and eating, and particularly let him alwayes haue his teeth and mouth so cleane, as they whom he shall entertain, may neuer receiue any annoyance by his breath."

Nicolas Faret, *The Honest Man*

Good news, gents! You don't have be gorgeous. Just check that your apparel isn't filthy, and—I know this is asking a lot—try to remember to dry your hair.

# *How to Make Yourself Invisible*

## ~

## 1560

"If thou wilt be made inuisible. Take the stone, which is called Ophethalmius, and wrappe it in the leafe of the Laurell, or Baye tree, & it is called Lapis obtelmicus, whose color is not named, for it is of many colours, and it is of such vertu, that it blindeth the sightes of them that stand about."

*The Boke of Secretes of Albertus Magnus*

At last, the secret of invisibility: just decorate yourself with foliage and shiny opals, and bystanders will be too dazzled by your bling to see you—or anything else.

# How to Put Out a Fire

~

## twelfth century

"If a fire blazes up, it should be extinguished with sand and bran, if it blazes up further, put on sand soaked in urine."

*Mappae clavicula*

Bonfire safety tip: presoak some sand in urine.

# *How to Whiten Your Teeth*

~

## 1686

"A Dentrifice to whiten the Teeth. Take of Harts-horn and horses Teeth, of each 2 ounces, Sea-shells, common Salt, Cypress-Nuts, each one Ounce; burn them together in an Oven, and make a powder, and work it up with the mucilage of Gum Tragacanth, and rub the Teeth therewith."

Hannah Woolley, *The Accomplish'd Lady's Delight*

And now you know how whitening toothpaste is made.

# How to Charm a Man

~

## 1896

"When you desire to make any one 'love' you with whom you meet, although not personally acquainted with him, you can very readily reach him and make his acquaintance…Wherever or whenever you meet again, at the first opportunity grasp his hand in an earnest, sincere, and affectionate manner, observing at the same time the following important directions, viz.: As you take his bare hand in yours, press your thumb gently, though firmly, between the bones of the thumb and the forefinger of his hand, and at the very instant when you press thus on the blood vessels (which you can before ascertain to pulsate) look him earnestly and lovingly in the eyes, and send all your heart's, mind's, and soul's strength into his organization, and he will be your friend…"

*The Ladies' Book of Useful Information*

This handy technique allows you not only to seduce an alluring stranger, but also to check his resting heart rate.

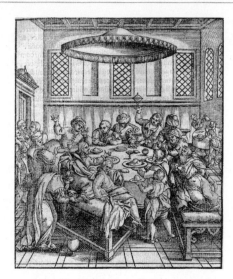

# *How to Sit at the Table*

~

## 1530

"Make sure that you do not bother the person sitting next to you with your feet. Squirming in your seat, and sitting now on one buttock and now the other, gives the impression that you are farting or trying to fart. Therefore, your body should remain upright and balanced."

Desiderius Erasmus, *De civilitate morum puerilium*

Further guidance on flatulence from the Prince of Humanists: the only thing worse than being exposed as a dinner-table farter is being wrongfully suspected.

# How to Make Chocolate

~

## 1685

"Take seven hundred Cacao Nuts, a pound and a half of white Sugar, two ounces of Cinnamon, fourteen grains of Mexico Pepper, call'd Chile or Pimiento, half an ounce of Cloves, three little Straws or Vanilla's de Campeche, or for want thereof, as much Annis Seed as will equal the weight of a shilling, or Achiot a small quantity as big as a Filbeard, which may be sufficient only to give it a colour; some add thereto Almonds, Filbeards, and the Water of Orange Flowers."

Philippe Sylvestre Dufour, *The Manner of Making of Coffee, Tea and Chocolate*

What are you waiting for? Those seven hundred cacao nuts aren't going to count themselves.

# *How to Stay Young*

~

## 1489

"There is a common and ancient opinion that certain prophetic women who are popularly called 'screech-owls' suck the blood of infants as a means, insofar as they can, of growing young again. Why shouldn't our old people…likewise suck the blood of a youth?—a youth, I say who is willing, healthy, happy and temperate, whose blood is of the best but perhaps too abundant. They will suck, therefore, like leeches, an ounce or two from a scarcely-opened vein of the left arm; they will immediately take an equal amount of sugar and wine; they will do this when hungry and thirsty and when the moon is waxing."

Marsilio Ficino, *De vita libri tres*

Wanted: one willing youth to participate in rejuvenation experiment. Hours flexible, but must be available at mealtimes when moon is waxing.

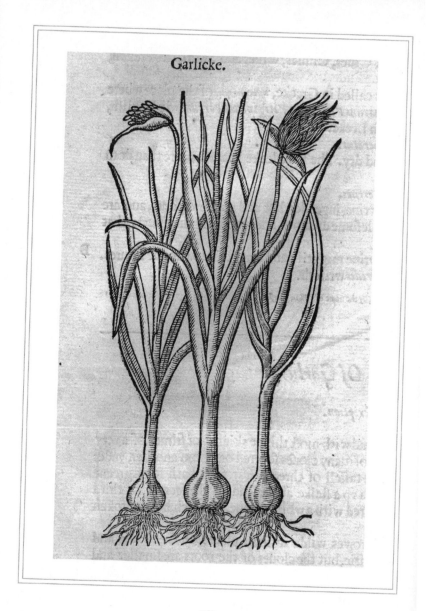

Garlicke.

# *How to Stay Healthy*

~

## 1607

"Six things that heere in order shall insue,
Against all poysons haue a secret poure.
Peares, Garlick, Reddish-roots, Nuts, Rape, & Rew,
But Garlicke cheefe, for they that it deuoure,
May drink, and care not who their drink do brew
May walke in ayres infected euery houre:
Sith Garlicke then hath poure to saue from death,
Beare with it though it make vnsauoury breath:
And scorne not Garlicke like to some, that think
It onely makes men winke, and drinke, and stink."

John Harrington, *The Englishmans Docter*

A steady diet of garlic will render you immune to poison, pestilence,
and death. In fact, it will protect you from just about everything
except your own stench.

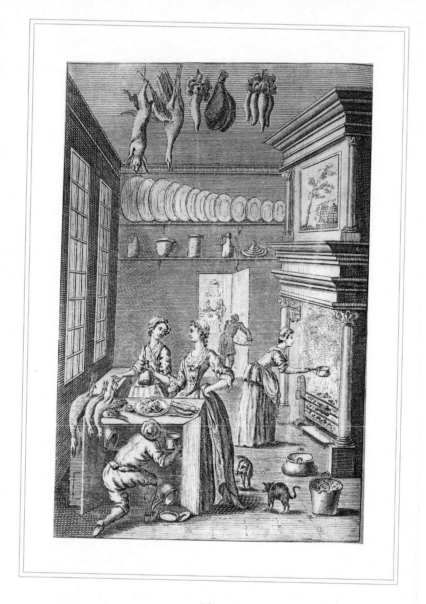

# *How to* c*M*ake *K*etchup

~

## 1774

"To make catchup to keep twenty years. Take a gallon of strong stale beer, one pound of anchovies washed from the pickle, a pound of shalots, peeled, half an ounce of mace, half an ounce of cloves, a quarter of an ounce of whole pepper, three or four large races of ginger, two quarts of the large mushroom⁄flaps rubbed to pieces. Cover all this close, and let it simmer till it is half wasted, then strain it through a flannel⁄bag; let it stand till it is quite cold, then bottle it. You may carry it to the Indies."

Hannah Glasse, *The Art of Cookery*

Planning a twenty-year sea voyage to the Indies, but unsure which condiments to pack? This mushroomy ketchup will sustain and console you for decades.

# How to Put the Moves on a Man

~

## C. 1250

"Sometimes, as I have said, when love is not fulfilled, the fault lies with the lady; for she may love a gentleman, and yet he may not know it. Here is what she must do if such be the case. She must call his attention to herself in any number of ways: by speaking to him of some vague concern; by feigning love in obvious jest; by long, affectionate glances; or by pleasant, courteous speech. In short, by anything but a frank and open entreaty. For I shall never deem it proper that woman be the pursuer and man the pursued. And yet, she may affect all other artful guises to disclose her love. If the man is so dim-witted that he fails to perceive it, so much the worse for him."

Richard de Fournival, *Consaus d'amours*

Ladies, when you really want to turn up the heat, say something vague or stare intensely. Just don't admit you're interested.

# How to Light a Fire

~

## 1612

"An easie way to procure Fire speedily. Take a round Glasse, and fill it with faire Water, and set it against the Sunne, so that it may stand fast: then take something that is very dry, and hold it neere the Glasse, (betweene the glasse and the Sun) and it will set the thing so holden on fire: (which is very strange to behold), the rather because fire which is an hot and dry Element, is procured out of water, which is a colde and moist Element."

*The Booke of Pretty Conceits*

This is a great trick if you can get the angle just right. If not, though, you'll still end up with a nice glass of lukewarm water. Win!

 *How to Put Out a Fire, twelfth century, page 153.*

# *How to Compliment a Lady*

~

## 1663

Amorous compliments endorsed by John Gough, *The Academy of Complements*:

"Her Dove-like eyes."
"Liquorous rolling eyes."
"Her cheeks shine like sparkling stones."
"Her Cheeks are like Punick Apples."
"Her Cheeks are spread with Spices and Flowers."
"Her breasts are the soft Pillows of love."
"Her breasts are soft and tender as the Pelican's."
"Her Thighes are fit subjects for the pleasant Songs of youthfull Poets to acquaint the world with."
"Her legs as stately and firm as marble pillars."

Looking to stand out on Tinder? Try the pelican line—it really gives you that element of surprise.

# How to Know If Death Is Imminent

~

## fifth century

"If there is pain in the nose, and if on the left side there are thick red [patches] without pain, and if [the patient] consistently desires vegetables, he will die on the twenty-fifth day."

Pseudo-Hippocrates, *Capsula eburnea*

I hate to break it to you. The occasional tomato, maybe a side salad with your burger? Fine. But *consistent* desire for vegetables? Better update your will.

 *How to Tell If Someone Is or Is Not Dead, c. 1380,* page 3.

# *How to Know If You're Pregnant*

~

## 1685

"To know if a Woman be with Child. Take her Urine and put it in a Copper⹅Pot, wherein put a piece of Iron filed bright, all Night: if she be with Child, you will see red Spots; if not, it will become black and rusty."

*Modern Curiosities of Art and Nature*

The seventeenth century: when men were men, women were tough, and using a home pregnancy test required skill in metallurgy.

☞ *How to Have a Beautiful Child, 1697,* page 99. ☜

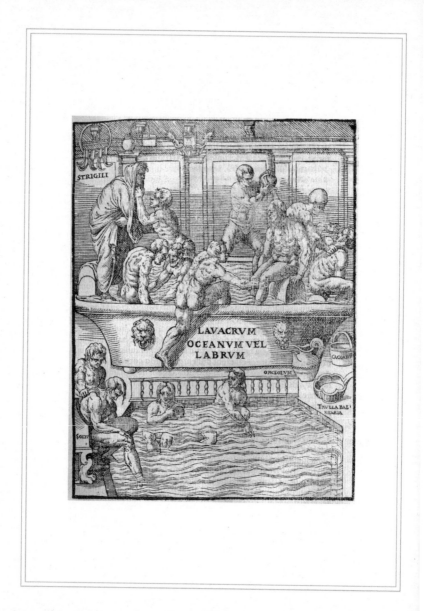

# How to Wash Your Head

~

## 1612

"You shall finde it wonderfull expedient, if you bath your head foure times in the yeare, and that with hot lee made of ashes. After which, you must cause one presently to poure two or three gallons of cold fountain water vpon your head. Then let your head be dryed with cold towels. Which sodaine pouring downe of cold water, although it doth mightily terrifie you, yet neuertheles, it is very good, for therby the naturall heate is stirred within the body, baldnesse is kept backe, and the memory is quickened."

William Vaughan, *Approved Directions for Health*

Believe it or not, the dreaded quarterly headwashing has its benefits.

☞ *How to Wash Your Hair, twelfth century,* page 68. ☜

# *How to Make a Hedgehog*

~

## 1725

"To make a Hedge-Hog. Take a Quart of New Cream and boil it, then beat an Egg and put into it, and take a quarter of a Pint of sowre Cream, and mix them well together, stirring it continually; let it boil till it be a little turn'd, then put it into a Cloth, and squeeze the Whey from it; when it's cold, mix it with pounded Almonds, and refin'd Sugar; then lay it like a Hedge-hog, and stick it with Almonds, cut small, and put good Cream about it; stick two or three Currans for the Nose and Eyes."

Robert Smith, *Court Cookery*

Sometimes you want to serve a hedgehog, but you can't find one at the farmers' market or dietary restrictions stand in your way. Enter the Hedge-Log: part cheese ball, part Mrs. Tiggy-Winkle, all eighteenth-century genius.

# *How to Avoid the Plague*

~

## 1579

"Whosoeuer eateth two Walnuts, two Fygs, twentie leaues of Rew, and one graine of Salt, all stampt and mixt together, fasting: shall bee safe from poyson and plague that daye."

Thomas Lupton, *A Thousand Notable Things*

This early modern energy bar provides the nutrients you need to get through a pestilential and poisonous workday. (NB: As instructed, take this with a grain of salt.)

# How to Be a Baroness

~

## 1404

"The knowledge of a baroness must be so comprehensive that she can understand everything…Moreover, she must have the courage of a man. This means that she should not be brought up overmuch among women nor should she be indulged in extensive and feminine pampering…she must conduct herself with such wisdom that she will be both feared and loved…She must be a good speaker, proud when pride is needed; circumspect with the scornful, surly, or rebellious; and charitably gentle and humble toward her good, obedient subjects…No one should ever be able to say of her that she acts merely to have her own way. Again, she should have a man's heart. She must know the laws of arms and all things pertaining to warfare, even prepared to command her men if there is need of it."

Christine de Pizan, *Le trésor de la cité des dames*

The baroness: a creature with the courage of a man, the wisdom of a woman, and the ass-kicking résumé of an archangel.

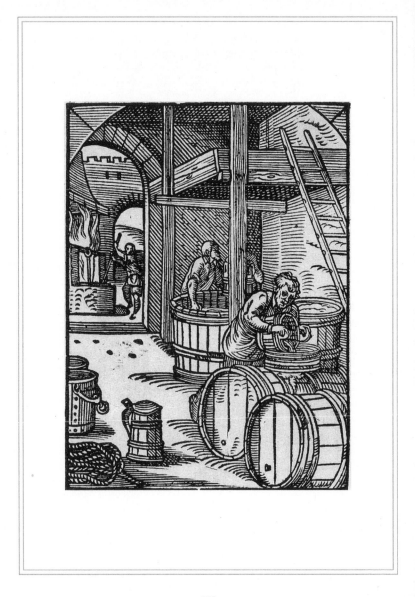

# How to Make Cock Ale

~

## 1697

"To make Cock Ale. Take nine Gallons of Ale, and let it Work; and when done Working, have in readiness four pound of Raisins of the Sun, stoned and bruised in a Mortar, two Nutmegs, and as much Mace bruised; then take two Cocks…break their Bones, and bruise them in a Mortar, so put them in a Vessel to your Ale, (before you put in all the Blade Fruit and Spice,) so stop them close: let it stand a Fortnight; and when you Bottle it, put in every Bottle two or three bits of Limon Peel, and as much candied Ginger Root, with a Lump of Sugar; stop it close: let it stand a Fortnight or three Weeks, then drink it; it is very pleasant, and good against Consumption."

*A New Book of Knowledge*

Some days, you're not sure whether you need a mug of ale or a steaming bowl of chicken broth. On those days, Cock Ale will drown your sorrows and cure your consumption.

# How to Make Macaroni and Cheese

## c. 1390

"Macrons. Make a thin leaf of dough and carve it into pieces, and put them into boiling water and boil it well. Take cheese and grate it, and melted butter, put [them] above and below…and serve forth."

*The Forme of Cury*

Need a quick weeknight dinner the kids will actually eat? These medieval macaroni practically serve themselves forth.

 *How to Make a Cheesy Omelet, c. 1393, page 135.*

# How to Serve a Live Bird at a Feast

~

## c. 1450

"Get a chicken or any other bird you want, and pluck it alive cleanly in hot water. Then get the yolks of 2 or 3 eggs; they should be beaten with powdered saffron and wheat flour, and distempered with fat broth or with the grease that drips under a roast into the dripping pan. By means of a feather glaze and paint your pullet carefully with this mixture so that its colour looks like roast meat. With this done, and when it is about to be served to the table, put the chicken's head under its wing, and turn it in your hands, rotating it until it is fast asleep. Then set it down on your platter with the other roast meat. When it is about to be carved it will wake up and make off down the table upsetting jugs, goblets and whatnot."

*The Vivendier*

Is your holiday turkey routine getting dull? This year, don't roast the bird—just denude, glaze, hypnotize, and serve. Plus, you will probably never be asked to host again. Win-win.

# How to Make a Cooked Bird Sing

~

## C. 1450

"To Make that Chicken Sing when it is dead and roasted, whether on the spit or in the platter. Take the neck of your chicken and bind it at one end and fill it with quicksilver and ground sulphur, filling until it is roughly half full; then bind the other end, but not too tightly. When you want it to sing, [heat] your neck or chicken. When it is quite hot, and when the mixture heats up, the air that is trying to escape will make the chicken's sound. The same can be done with a gosling, with a piglet and with any other birds. And if it doesn't cry loudly enough, tie the two ends more tightly."

*The Vivendier*

From the same geniuses who brought you the live bird entrée, this sequel recipe will provide a soundtrack for your feast! And what's a feast without some toxic, mercury-based stuffing?

# How to Cure Lovesickness

~

## eleventh century

"What better helps erotic lovers so that they do not sink into excessive thoughts: temperate and fragrant wine is to be given; listening to music; conversing with dearest friends; recitation of poetry; looking at bright, sweet-smelling and fruitful gardens having clear running water; walking or amusing themselves with good-looking women or men."

Constantinus Africanus, *Viaticum*

Recovering from a bad breakup? Drink some wine, call your best friend, and then go find some hot new women or men to play with.

# How to Win a Legal Case

~

C. 1260

"If someone carries with him the teeth, skin, and eyes of a wolf, he will be victorious at court if he has a lawyer and he will be rich among all nations."

Albertus Magnus, *De animalibus*

A smart motto for life: carry wolf teeth, but always hire a lawyer.

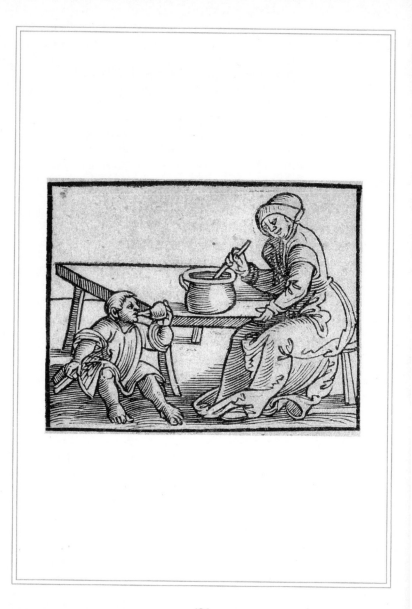

# How to Feed Your Child

~

## 1692

"As to his *Meals*, I should think it best that, as much as it can
be conveniently avoided, they should not be kept constantly to
an hour. For when custom has fixed his eating to certain stated
periods, his stomach will expect victuals at the usual hour and
grow peevish if he passes it... Therefore I would have no time
kept constantly to for his breakfast, dinner, and supper, but rather
varied almost every day. And if between these, which I call *meals*,
he will eat, let him have, as often as he calls for it, good dry bread.
If anyone think this too hard and sparing a diet for a child, let
them know that a child will never starve nor dwindle for want of
nourishment who, besides flesh at dinner, and spoonmeat or some
such other thing, at supper, may have good bread and beer as
often as he has a stomach."

John Locke, *Some Thoughts Concerning Education*

Child-rearing advice from the Father of Liberalism. To nourish your
child properly, you will need: (1) dry bread, (2) plenty of beer, and (3)
the element of surprise.

☞ *How to Serve Wine to Your Toddler, c. 1450*, page 105. ☜

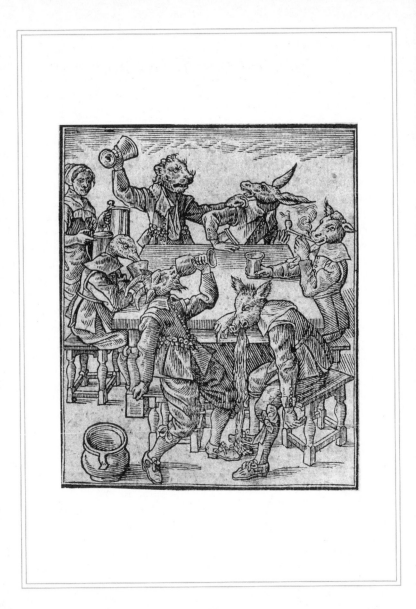

# How to Prevent Drunkenness

~

## 1653

"How to prevent drunkenness. Drink first a good large draught of Sallet Oyl, for that will float upon the Wine which you shall drink, and suppresse the spirits from ascending into the brain. Also what quantity soever of new milk you drink first, you may well drink thrise as much wine after, without danger of being drunk. But how sick you shal be with this prevention, I wil not here determine."

Hugh Plat, *The Jewel House of Art and Nature*

The recipe for a foolproof anti-drunkenness cocktail: three parts wine, one part milk, a dash of salad oil. Shake well and immediately reconsider.

☞ *How to Sober Up, 1612*, page 18. 🖐

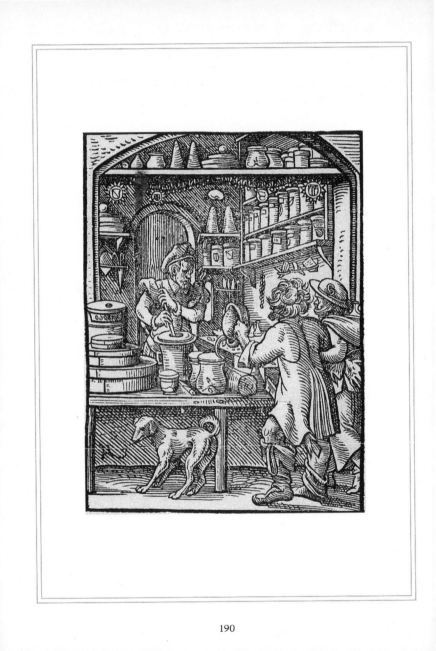

# *How to Cure a Headache*

~

## 1561

"A wounderfull experience for the headacke. Set a dish or platter of tynne vpon the bare head filled with water, putte an vnce and an halfe, or two vnces of molten leade therein, whyle he hath it vpon the head. Or els make a garlande of Veruayne, and wear it Daye and night, that helpeth wounderfully."

Hieronymus Brunschwig, *A Most Excellent and Perfecte Homish Apothecarye*

The problem with most headache remedies is that they aren't enough like performance art. Melting metal on your head while festooned with herbs: now *that* is a *wounderfull* experience.

 *How to Cure a Headache, ninth century,* page 33.

# *How to Sleep*

~

## 1474

"It is very good to sleep first on the right side, then on the left. No sane person should sleep on his back, for many serious illnesses result, since liquid humor, when turned from its proper course by such a position in bed, may infect brain and nerves and kidneys… At night we must avoid the moon, especially when sleeping, for it stirs cold humors and generates many kinds of catarrhs, especially if the moon's rays, which are cold and damp, fall on the head of the sleeper."

Bartolomeo Platina, *De honesta voluptate et valetudine*

This sleep choreography is a little fiddly, but you can thank Platina when you avoid a brain infection.

☞ *How to Cure Insomnia, 1597,* page 76. ☜

G.V.<sup>en</sup>Gucht Sculp.

# *How to Protect Your Infant*

~

## 1697

"Great care must be taken that the child be not frightened, and it must never be left alone, lest it be injured, by venemous Creatures, or some other external injuries, which they cannot resist, for it is known that Scorpions, Serpents, and such like Creatures have crept into Childrens mouths, or other wise injured them, or Cats by lying upon them have suffocated them."

John Pechey, *A General Treatise of the Diseases of Infants and Children*

Hello, new parent! The seventeenth century would like to remind you that a whole army of scorpions, snakes, and maniacal housecats is just waiting for a chance to jump into that crib. Good luck sleeping now!

☞ *How to Raise Your Child, twelfth century,* page 57. ☜

# How to Keep Your Hands Warm

~

## 1579

"Whosoeuer annoynts his feete or hands, with the grease of a Woolfe: he shall not be hurt with any colde of his handes, or feete so annointed."

Thomas Lupton, *A Thousand Notable Things*

Mittens or wolf grease: the choice is yours.

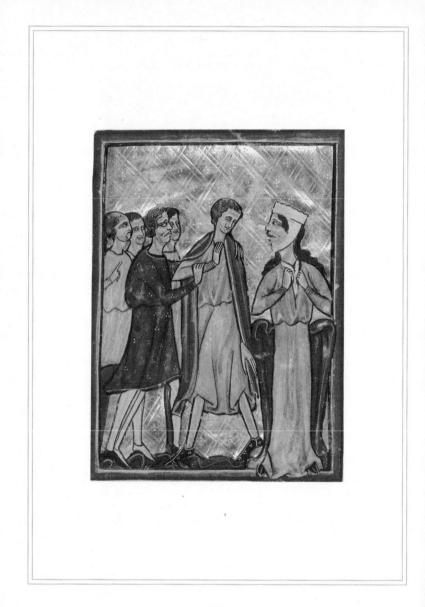

# *How to Turn Down Your Lord's Wife*

~

## C. 1200

"If your lord's wife frequently turns her eyes toward you, and aims shameful sparks at you, letting you know that she'd like to sleep with you; if she says, 'the whole house, and my husband the lord will serve you forever, you alone will be my love, you will rule everything, all of the lord's things will lie open to you'...Listen to me, my son, keep in your heart what I advise you. Between two evils choose the lesser, son: the best plan is to pretend you are ill, fake some pains, and leave wisely and prudently."

Daniel of Beccles, *Urbanus magnus*

Take it from the Middle Ages: you can *always* pretend you ate some tainted pottage or hurt your back in a boar hunt.

# How to Look Good While Dancing

~

## 1538

"When you are dancing, always maintain an agreeable face and please, brother, wear a pleasant expression. Some men, when they are dancing, always look as if they are weeping and as if they want to crap hard turds."

Antonius Arena, *Leges dansandi*

Look, we've all got problems, but *please* try not to bring yours onto the dance floor, especially if they involve bowel movements.

# How to Cure Head Congestion

~

## 1596

"A Medicine for the stopping of the nose and head, which commeth by reason of colde. Take a good quantity of the iuice of Primrose, and blow it with a quill into the Patients nose, and let him keepe himselfe warme after it, and it will cleare both his head and nose."

*A Rich Store-House or Treasury for the Diseased*

Your patient may be alarmed when you stick a quill into his nose and pressure wash his sinuses with primrose juice, but he'll thank you later.

# How to Make a Christmas Pie

~

## 1774

"To make a Yorkshire Christmas Pie. First make a good standing crust, let the wall and bottom be very thick; bone a turkey, a goose, a fowl, a partridge, and a pigeon, Season them all very well, take half an ounce of mace, half an ounce of nutmegs, a quarter of an ounce of cloves, and half an ounce of black pepper, all beat fine together, two large spoonfuls of salt, and then mix them together. Open the fowls all down the back, and bone them; first the pigeon, then the partridge; cover them; then the fowl, then the goose, and then the turkey, which must be large; season them all well first, and lay them in the crust, so as it will look only like a whole turkey; then have a hare ready cased, and wiped with a clean cloth. Cut it to pieces, that is, joint it; season it, and lay it as close as you can on one side; on the other side woodcocks, moor game, and what sort of wild fowl you can get. Season them well, and lay them close; put at least four pounds of butter into the pie, then lay on your lid, which must be a very thick one, and let it be well baked. It must have a very hot oven, and will take at least four hours."

Hannah Glasse, *The Art of Cookery*

Holiday dining doesn't get more efficient than this Christmas pie. Just toss in your calling birds, French hens, turtle doves, and the partridge in a pear tree. You could probably fit a few lords a-leaping in there, too, if you've got those on hand.

# How to Improve Your Memory

## 1563

"To make one haue a good memorie. Take a Tooth or the lefte legge of a Badgre…and binde it aboute youre riggt arme nexte vnto the flesh. Take also the gall of a Partrich, and rubbe your temples with it that it maie soke into the skin and fleshe, ones in a moneth, and it will make you haue a good memorie."

Alessio Piemontese, *The Second Part of the Secretes of Maister Alexis of Piemont*

This is a bit of a Faustian bargain, isn't it? Your improved memory comes at the cost of having to adorn yourself with badger parts and partridge goo. Well, at least others will definitely remember *you*.

# How to Kiss

~

## 1777

"Some authors will have it, that a kiss is no kiss, or at best a half one, unless returned at the same time…its signification is determined by the circumstances, the degree of warmth, the part, the time, and other particulars needless to enumerate. But of all kisses, the turtle-billing one is the most emphatic, but rarely used, where there is not full liberty to use every thing else."

*A Dictionary of Love, With Notes*

Next time you need to interpret the signification of a kiss, take careful notes on the degree of warmth, the time, and the … part.

# How to Care for Your Dog

~

## C. 1393

"As soon as you arrive home, be diligent that you yourself or your men ahead of you feed the dogs well, then give them fresh clean water in a basin to drink. Next have them put to bed on nice straw in a warm place, in front of the fire if they are wet or muddy...
If you act this way, they will not pester people at the table or sideboard and they will not get into the beds. If you do not care for their needs well, know that when they have worked hard and are hungry, they will scrounge under the table or seize a piece of meat from the sideboard or the kitchen, and they will snap at each other and cause upsets to provide for their needs. In so doing they tire themselves and do not rest at all, and thus remain beggars and badly behaved, and this is your fault, not theirs."

*Le Ménagier de Paris*

Wet, muddy dog in your bed again? The Middle Ages warned you.

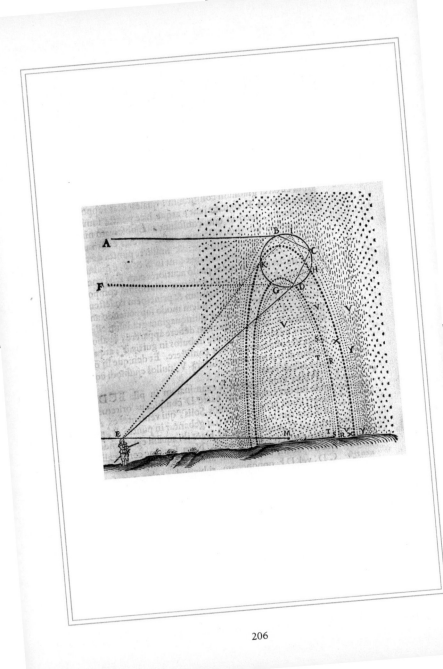

# How to Make a Rainbow

~

## 1633

"The Rainebow is a thing admirable in the world, which ravisheth
often the eyes and spirits of men in consideration of his rich
intermingled colours which are seene under the cloudes, seeming
as the glistering of the starres, pretious stones, & ornaments of
the most beautious flowers...I will shew you how you may doe
it at your doore, by a fine and facill experiment. Take water in
your mouth, and turne your backe to the Sunne, and your face
against some obscure place, then blow out the water which is in
your mouth, that it may bee sprinkled in small drops and vapours:
you shall see these atomes vapours in the beames of the Sunne to
turne into a faire Rainebow, but all the griefe is that it lasteth not
but soone is vanished."

Hendrik van Etten, *Mathematicall Recreations*

Just make sure that no one is standing directly in the path of your
beauteous mouth rainbow.

two profugus pro in italiam. Terentius in eunucho. Ar ille mnos uenit
natus scedei. pro ante sederit. frequentissima est h figura. ap auctores
in quia postea desint. naui o e n qd est ablco eiruinos pro in loco poni
to octui tri sit haurire. Melius est th distinguend. et uoc. etiam un
aloco accipit. naui o e n. Ab humo. Nos genitiuo qn in loco ablatiuo
et deloco. et aclatiuo ap locu inimur. humi sum. Saluti in iugurtino
que humi ande ait. arenoso gignunt. Virgili th erectu liroze dif
unberis. quatuor quida distinguentes erectu ad co. sequens libu dif
unoze egentem suscepit. et regni demens in parte locaui. Ex p t no
nenoie a a m y m e h o y tpy pe. kai to p e k o n. Simile Virgili in
iii. georgicon. Pascunt u siluas et sima uoci. Idem in iii. eneid. Impl
eat et miseros morsu depasceretur artus. Sic ergo possum dicere. sanos
illui rei et illa re. Terentii in adelphis. Sed pequam unus sum om
niu reru sanior.

# *How to Handle Books*

~

## 1345

"The race of scholars is commonly badly brought up, and unless they are bridled in by the rules of their elders they indulge in infinite puerilities... You may happen to see some headstrong youth lazily lounging over his studies, and when the winter's frost is sharp, his nose running from the nipping cold drips down, nor does he think of wiping it with his pocket,handkerchief until he has bedewed the book before him with the ugly moisture....He does not fear to eat fruit or cheese over an open book, or carelessly to carry a cup to and from his mouth...

But the handling of books is specially to be forbidden to those shameless youths, who as soon as they have learned to form the shapes of letters, straightway, if they have the opportunity, become unhappy commentators, and wherever they find an extra margin about the text, furnish it with monstrous alphabets, or if any other frivolity strikes their fancy, at once their pen begins to write it."

Richard de Bury, *Philobiblon*

Hello, reader! This head-cold season, please remember that your book is not a Kleenex. Also, medieval manuscripts and cheese are not a great combination.

# How to Sweet-Talk Your Lady

~

## 1656

"Instructions for Lovers: teaching them, how to demean themselves towards their Sweet-hearts. You must not accost them with a shrug, as if you were lowsie: With, 'your Ladie', 'best Ladie', or 'most super-excellent Ladie': neither must you let your words come rumbling forth, ushered in with a good full mouth'd, Oath, as 'I love you'…
But you must in fine gentle words, deliver your true affection: praise your Mistress Eies, her Lip, her Chin, her Nose, her Neck, her Face, her Hand, her Feet, her Leg, her Waste, her every thing."

*Cupids Master-piece*

A few choice compliments, and that super-excellent lady will be yours. Careful with that seventeenth-century spelling, though: it's her *waist* you want to praise.

# How to Get Pregnant

~

## 1671

"The heart of a male Quail born about the man, and the heart of the female about the woman furthers conception, and creates love between the man and his wife."

William Sermon, *The Ladies Companion*

What could be sweeter than "his" and "hers" quail hearts? They're like matching lockets for quail lovers!

👉 *How to Know If You're Pregnant, 1685*, page 171. 👈

# *How to Harvest Melons*

~

## 1691

"You must not think it much to visit your *Meloniere* at the least four times a day, when your Melons begin to ripen, least they pass their Prime, and loose of their Tempting, becoming lank and fleshy."

Nicolas de Bonnefons, *The French Gardiner*

The melon farmer must approach his crop like a cougar stalking its prey, waiting in the shadows for the perfect opportunity to pounce.

# How to Predict Bad Weather

~

## C. 1470

"When you see a cat sitting in the sun in a window, licking its behind and rubbing its ear with its leg, be sure that it will rain that very day."

*Les Evangiles des Quenouilles*

The good news is that this forecasting technique requires nothing more than your cat. The bad news is that it is almost certainly going to rain every day.

# How to Care for a Newborn

~

## 1256

"After the woman has delivered the child, you should know how to take care of the child. Know that as soon as the child is born, it should be wrapped in crushed roses mixed with fine salt...And when one wishes to swaddle [the baby], the members should be gently couched and arranged so as to give them a good shape, and this is easy for a wise nurse; for just as wax when it is soft takes whatever form one wishes to give to it, so also the child takes the form which its nurses give to it. And for this reason, you should know that beauty and ugliness are due in large measure to nurses. And when its arms are swaddled, and the hands over the knees, and the head lightly swaddled and covered, let it sleep in the cradle."

Aldobrandino of Siena, *Le régime du corps*

Caring for a newborn is a bit like curing a ham. Just salt it with some aromatics, arrange it nicely, and wait for it to age.

☞ *How to Wash a Baby, 1744*, page 229. ☜

# How to Leave a Party

~

## C. 1200

"When you are about to leave, have your horse at the door; don't mount your horse in the hall, unless the host tells you to."

Daniel of Beccles, *Urbanus magnus*

It's good to know how to make an exit, but leaping on a horse while you're still indoors is a little dramatic.

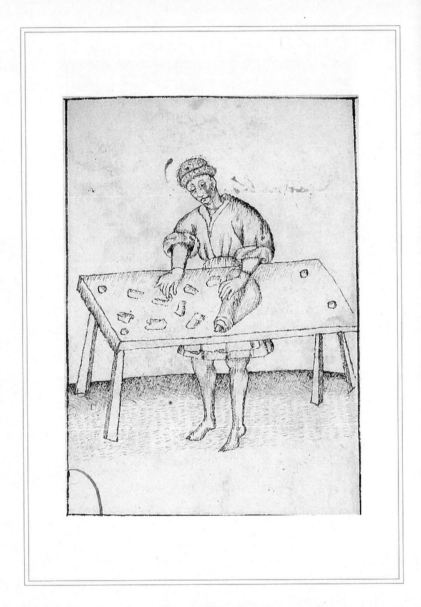

216

# *How to Make Tagliatelle*

~

## 1570

"Work two pounds of flour, three eggs and warm water into a dough, kneading it on a table for a quarter of an hour. Roll it out thin with a pin and let the sheet of dough dry out a little. With a cutting wheel trim away the irregular parts, the fringes. When it has dried, though not too much because it would break up, sprinkle it with flour through the sifter so it will not stick. Then take the rolling pin and, beginning at one end, wrap the whole sheet loosely onto the pin, draw the pin out and cut the rolled-up dough crosswise with a broad, thin knife. When they are cut, broaden them. Let them dry out a little and, when they are dry, filter off the excess flour through a sieve. Make up a soup of them with a fat meat broth, or milk and butter. When they are cooked, serve them hot with cheese, sugar and cinnamon. If you want to make lasagne of them, cut the dough lengthwise on the pin, and likewise divide it lengthwise in two, and cut that into little squares. Cook them in the broth of a hare, a crane or some other meat, or in milk. Serve them hot with cheese, sugar and cinnamon."

Bartolomeo Scappi, *Opera*

Perfect for those evenings when all you have in the pantry is flour, eggs, and an old jar of crane broth.

217

# *How to Groom Your Eyebrows*

~

1563

"Take the galle of a he Gote or of a she Gote, but the he Gote is better, and dooeth it soner, and rub youre eye browes, and the heare will shortly fall awaie."

Alessio Piemontese, *The Second Part of the Secretes of Maister Alexis of Piemont*

Why bother with plucking or waxing when you could have your eyebrows digested by goat enzymes? But remember to ask your salon for the superior he-goat gall.

# How to Cure Gas

~

## 1685

"Against the Wind in the Belly. Apply a living Tench to the Patients Navel, the Head being upwards towards the Stomach; and tye it fast on with a Napkin; and there leave it twenty four hours, till it be dead; then bury it in the Dung, and you will see the Wind will vanish."

Nicolas Lemery, *Modern Curiosities of Art and Nature*

If anyone asks why you have a dying fish strapped to your abdomen, just explain that it's for your wind problem. I *promise* they'll leave you alone.

*How to Fart, 1530,* page 9.

# *How to Wear Platform Shoes*

~

## 1600

"Now in order to walk nicely, and to wear chopines properly
on one's feet, so that they do not twist or go awry (for if one is
ignorant of how to wear them, one may splinter them, or fall
frequently, as has been and still is observed at parties and in
church), it is better for [the lady] to raise the toe of the foot
she moves first when she takes a step, for by raising it thus, she
straightens the knee of that foot, and this extension keeps her
body attractive and erect, besides which her chopine will not fall
off that foot. Also by thus raising it she avoids sliding it along
[the ground], nor does she make any unpleasant noise. Then she
should put it down, and repeat the same thing with the other foot
(which follows)...By walking this way, therefore, even if the lady's
chopines are more than a handbreadth-and-a-half high, she will
seem to be on chopines only three fingerbreadths high, and will be
able to dance *flourishes* and galliard variations at a ball, as I have
just shown the world this day."

Fabritio Caroso, *Nobiltà di dame*

Wear the boring flats, or risk a tumble in the sexy heels? Neither—just
follow these steps and you'll be gliding effortlessly a handsbreadth-
and-a-half above the crowd.

222

# *How to Adjust Your Posture*

~

## 1484

"How young maidens ought not to turn their heads thoughtlessly here and there. Daughters, don't be like the tortoise or the crane, which turn their faces and their heads above their shoulders, winding their heads here and there like a weathervane. Instead, hold yourselves steadfast like the hare, a beast that always looks in front of him without turning his head all about. Always look directly in front of you and if you must look to the side, turn your face and your body together, holding yourself firm and sure, for those who frivolously cast their eyes about and turn their faces here and there are mocked."

Geoffrey de la Tour Landry, *The Book of the Knight of the Tower*

Turning your whole body rather than just your head will give the impression that you are either trustworthy or suffering from a neck injury.

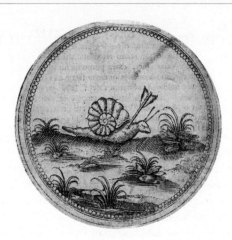

# *How to* Make *Snail Bread*

~

## 1685

"A sort of Bread, of which a Mouthful can maintain a Man eight daies, without eating any thing else. Take a quantity of Snails, and make them void their sliminess; then dry and reduce them to fine Powder, of which make a Loaf, with a Mouthful of which a Man may be eight days without eating."

Nicolas Lemery, *Modern Curiosities of Art and Nature*

One bite of this special bread and the idea of eating anything at all will nauseate you for eight days! The only problem: to learn how to make snails void their sliminess, you'll have to consult a different manual.

# *How to Use Bacon*

~

## C. 530

"As for raw bacon which, so I hear, the Franks have a habit of eating…they are healthier than other people because of this food. Let me give a good example so that what I am writing may be believed: thick bacon, placed for a long time on all wounds, be they external or internal or caused by a blow, both cleanses any putrefaction and aids healing. Look at what power there is in raw bacon, and see how the Franks heal what doctors try to cure with drugs or with potions."

Anthimus, *De obseruatione ciborum*

The bacon Band-Aid: it will save you a trip to the emergency room.

# How to Make a Quick Cocktail

~

## 1658

"How to make a speedy or present Drink that Travellers may brew for themselves, when they cannot rellish their Beer or Ale at their Innes. Take a quart of good water, put therein five or six spoonfuls of good Aqua-vitae, and an ounce of Sugar, with a branch of Rosemary, brew them a pretty while out of one pot into another, and then is your drink prepared."

John White, *A Rich Cabinet*

Just bring some simple syrup, aqua vitae, and rosemary when you travel, shake it up, and tell your innkeeper you'll pass on his nasty beer.

# How to Wake or Sleep

~

## 1685

"To make one wake or sleep. You must cut dexterously the Head of a Toad, alive, and at once, and let it dry, in observing that one Eye be shut, and the other open; that which is found open makes one wake, and that shut causes Sleep, by carrying it about one."

Nicolas Lemery, *Modern Curiosities of Art and Nature*

Who needs caffeine or Ambien when you've got the shriveled head of a winking toad?

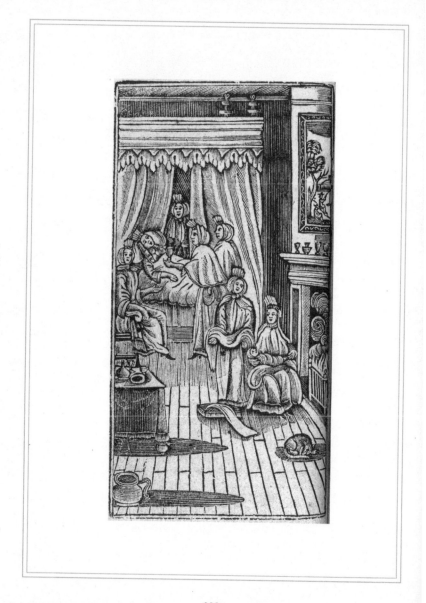

# How to Wash a Baby

~

## 1744

"Carry it to the Fire-Side, and cleanse it in the Manner following: Having got about a Pint of Wine (or, if the Circumstances of the Family be but mean, as much Small-Beer) dissolve in it a little fresh Butter, and with a Linen-Rag or Spunge dipt in it luke-warm, wash the Child's Body all over, beginning at the Head…and when you have finish'd the Head, put upon it a woolen Cap, to prevent its taking Cold, and then proceed to wash the rest of the Body; and all being done, wipe the Child dry with a fine warm Cloth, and wrap it up in Swadling Clothes….As soon as you have wrapp'd it up and dress'd it, lay it to sleep. Lay it not on its Back, but on one Side, that the Slime which flows from its Mouth, may have an easy Discharge. You may if you will give it a little Wine sweetened with fine Sugar now and then."

*The Nurse's Guide*

To bathe your new baby, you will need: wine, butter, and sugar. And when you have finished the bath and set the baby down to de-slime, you can fortify yourself with the leftover bath ingredients.

How to Change a Diaper, 1612, page 117.

# How to Soothe a Teething Baby

~

## c. 1450

"Sometimes babies have trouble with teething. In that case you should squeeze the gums with your fingers, and gently massage them, and the palate as well. And you should anoint the gums with the brains of a hare (which are very suitable for this purpose), or with fat or butter or good-quality olive oil; and you should do this twice a day. The milk of a dog is suitable, too. It is also very helpful to use hen's fat for both anointing and massaging the gums."

Michele Savonarola, *Ad mulieres ferrarienses*

Teething trouble? No problem—just smear the baby's mouth with some fatty goo. The only issue is that once he's tasted hare's brains, he'll never go back to pureed pears.

# *How to Escape from Prison*

~

## 1642

"The lens is of such efficacy in burning that it can not only burn wood and other materials suited to combustion, but it can also liquefy lead, tin, and other metals, just as you see in the figure on the right that the prisoner (A) secretly secures liberty for himself, as he points the lens (B) toward the sun, and liquefies the lead joints (C), with which the iron bars are fastened outside the walls, so that he may freely escape."

Mario Bettinus, *Apiaria universae philosophiae mathematicae*

Need to escape from a poorly constructed prison with lots of direct sunlight? Have a giant lens on hand? Problem solved.

# How to Wear Gentlemanly
# Underwear

~

## 1891

"Underclothing. This consists of shirt, drawers, and half-hose. The material may be flannel, balbriggan, or silk. White is the proper color, because it is pure and clean. Such colors as pink, or blue, or black may be worn. Have the drawers fit tight, or the trousers will set ill…Underclothing should be changed at least twice a day. Silk is worn always with evening dress."

Mortimer Delano de Lannoy, *Simplex Munditiis*

You can tell a gentleman by his evening drawers. They are silk. They are tight. They may be pink. And they are *extremely* fresh.

# How to Manage Your Nose

~

## 1640

"It also is plaine, that it is very ill, to be carelesse concerning thy nostrils, for there be some that breath very loud through them, and at times wipe them with their hands and then rub one hand against the other, at other times they thrust their fingers into their nostrils, and make Pellets of that they picke out, even before every body, that is present: as in like manner, some are wont to make cakes of the waxe, which they picke out of their ears, and into this carelesenesse and slovenlinesse we have observed many to fall."

Lucas Gracián Dantisco, *Galateo espagnol, or*
*The Spanish Gallant*

You know you're a real Gallant when you can resist making sculptures with your bodily secretions.

# How to Predict Cost of Living

~

C. 1470

"When you see wolves looking for their prey close to towns or in the villages, you should know that it is a sign of high cost of living to come."

*Les Evangiles des Quenouilles*

If you thought the recent spate of wolf attacks in the neighborhood would drive down property values, think again.

# How to Spit

~

## 1646

"Spet not far off thee, nor behinde thee, but a side, a little distant, and not right before thy companion: but if it be some grosse flegme, one ought if it may bee, tread upon it. Be spet not the windowes in the streets, nor spet on the fire, nor on a Bason, nor on any other place where the spettle cannot bee taken away, by putting thy foot thereon."

Francis Hawkins, *Youths Behavior*

The trick to public spitting is a nimble foot. It's preferable not to be-spet your companion, but if you do, just tread upon him discreetly.

# *How to Choose a Cook*

~

## 1474

"One should have a trained cook with skill and long experience, patient with his work and wanting especially to be praised for it. He should lack all filth and dirt and know in a suitable way the force and nature of meats, fish and vegetables so that he may understand what ought to be roasted, boiled, or fried. He should be alert enough to discern by taste what is too salty or too flat... he should not be gluttonous or greedy... so as not to appropriate and devour what his master was supposed to eat."

Bartolomeo Platina, *De honesta voluptate et valetudine*

Wanted: experienced cook, lacking filth, not gluttonous.

☞ *How to Be a Head Chef, 1473*, page 133. ☜

# *How to Dye Your Hair Green*

~

## 1563

"To dye Heare into a Greene coloure. Take freshe Capers, and distill theym, and washe your heare with the water of them in the sunne, and they will become greene."

Alessio Piemontese, *The Second Part of the Secretes of Maister Alexis of Piemont*

Going through a rebellious phase, or just need a quick DIY tree costume? Caper shampoo to the rescue!

# How to Keep Your Cat

~

## c. 1470

"If you have a good cat and you don't want to lose it, you must rub its nose and four legs with butter for three days, and it will never leave the house."

*Les Evangiles des Quenouilles*

This trick will certainly prevent your cat from running away. It's less clear whether the cat will stick around because of adoration or poor traction.

# How to Cure a Sore Throat

~

## 1685

"Take a Sheeps small Guts, put them about your Neck till they be cold; then apply others hot, from the Sheep new kill'd, and so continue this as long as you please."

Nicolas Lemery, *Modern Curiosities of Art and Nature*

How long will this please you? There's only one way to find out.

# How to Make a Turf Bench

~

## C. 1305

"Between the level turf and the herbs let there be a higher piece of turf made in the fashion of a seat, suitable for flowers and amenities; the grass in the sun's path should be planted with trees or vines, whose branches will protect the turf with shade and cast a pleasant refreshing shadow."

Piero de' Crescenzi, *Liber ruralium commodorum*

Why buy lawn furniture when your lawn could *be* furniture?

# How to Make a Poisoned Arrow

~

## twelfth century

"Another toxic substance, with which an arrow may be poisoned in battle. Take the sweat which appears between the hips of a horse on the right side, and dip the arrow in it. This has been properly proved."

*Mappae clavicula*

This sweaty poison was proven effective in a rigorous double-blind study.

# How to Know the Moon's Phase

~

## 1658

"Our common House-cats also have this property by the predomination that the Moon hath over them, that their Eye-brows do increase, or decrease each day according to the course of the Moon, and her aspects; wich thing is daily seen to him that pleaseth to note the experience thereof."

John White, *A Rich Cabinet*

Your cat is raising her eyebrows at you a little more each day because she cannot believe you are this gullible.

DO YOU PLEASE TO HAVE YOUR BED WARM'D SIR?

# *How to Cure Soreness*

~

## 1835

"To remove great stiffness or soreness after a hard day's ride or hunt. On going to bed, order a pan with bright glowing coals, throw a handful of brown sugar over them, with or without a few juniper berries; have your bed well warmed and fumigated with this sweet-scented steam from the sugar, which, instead of allowing to escape, you should creep into, whilst yet quite warm. All the soreness will have left your bones by the next morning."

Charles Random de Berenger, *Helps and Hints How to Protect Life and Property*

Sore from a hard day of hunting? Just slow-cook yourself with some aromatics, and you'll be tender and luscious in the morning.

# How to Mouse-Proof
## Your Cheese

~

1581

"How to make a Receit, that neither Rat nor Mouse shall eat or gnaw of your Cheese. The Weasel, the Rat, and Mouse, are at such deadly hatred one with the other, as that, if you put the brain of a Weasel into the Rennets or Curds whereof you intend to make your Cheese, neither Rats nor Mice will ever come to taste or eat thereof."

Thomas Hill, *Naturall and Artificiall Conclusions*

With this clever recipe, your cheese will finally be safe from gnawing vermin. Wait until after the cheese course, though, to tell your dinner guests the secret of your wondrous weasel cheese.

# *How to Behave at School*

~

## 1595

"Be it far from thee to go vnto the Schoole with as ill a will as wicked dooers goe vnto the Stockes, or to the Gallowes…when thou art at Schoole, bee studious in thy lectures learning, attentiue to thy Masters wordes and documents, what soeuer thy Master shall teach, mark it heedfully, and meditate thereon earnestly vntill thou haue learned the same perfectlye…Flie all fighting and wrangling with thy fellowes. But be curteous, gentle & lowlie, among all both rich and poore. Make no noyse nor vse any meane, whereby thou maiest disturbe thy schoolefellowes: much lesse thy schoolemaster."

William Fiston, *The Schoole of Good Manners*

Also: yield not to the temptations of Facebook during thy lectures, do not rely overmuch on Wikipedia for thy term paper, and mock not thy Master on social media.

# *How to Live*

~

"May joyful songs often gladden your soul. Cultivate pleasant words, not quarrelsome. May you often have attractive new clothes, and may you sometimes have a generous companion in bed. Avoid pillows stuffed with bran or hair, and those that are dirty. Consume platters of delicious food and undiluted wine. Don't overindulge the appetite; scorn the glutton. Strive to be well-mannered, stay away from vices, and take care to avoid the things that are dangerous to you. If your skin is mangy, ask your doctor. Often have sweet music for your ears. Seek prosperity for yourself, be faithful, stay away from deceit. Flee envy; don't let peevish anger seize you. When you are in holy places, cultivate sanctity. Let dirty words and shameful deeds be detestable to you. Let your actions always be forthright, never shady. Thus you will live long in splendid and happy times."

Daniel of Beccles, *Urbanus magnus*

The medieval keys to good living: print them out (by hand, of course) and hang them on the wall of your castle. And get that mange checked out.

# Acknowledgments

When it comes to hiccup cures, The Past has much to offer. But this project has also profited from the expertise of The Present:

I am grateful to many friends, family, colleagues, neighbors, and readers who know How to Admire Old Books. Andrew Crabtree, Carol Chiodo, and Jared Banks provided early encouragement; Morris Tichenor shared expertise about filthy Latin; the Johns Hopkins Mellon seminar participants theorized about historical curiosities after-hours; Peabody colleagues, including Mark Janello, Paul Mathews, and Sebastian Vogt, offered inspiration; and Hollis Robbins demonstrated How to Ask the Best Questions.

I am grateful to the librarians, curators, and scholars who know How to Care For Old Books. Many people made their collections and expertise available and turned pages on my behalf, including Lynley Herbert at the Walters; Elizabeth Frengel and Aaron T. Pratt, who assisted my research at Yale; and Paul Espinosa, Heidi Herr, and Earle Havens at Johns Hopkins.

I am grateful to the people who know How to Make New Books. This one came into being thanks to the vision and dedication of my agent, Jim Gill, and Paul Whitlatch, Megan Gerrity, and the team at Hachette.

Finally, I am grateful to my husband, Jim Coleman, who knows How to Encourage Asking the Past in All Ways, Including but Not Limited to Scholarly Advice, Witticisms, and Pizza; and to Eleanor, who knows How to Stay in the Present.

# Notes

*How to Adjust Your Posture*, 1484:

Geoffrey de la Tour Landry, *The Book of the Knight of the Tower*, trans. Rebecca
    Barnhouse, *The Book of the Knight of the Tower: Manners for Young Medieval
    Women*, (New York, 2006), 79.
Geoffrey de la Tour Landry's *Livre pour l'enseignement de ses filles (Book for the
    Instruction of his Daughters)* of 1371 was translated into English by William
    Caxton in 1484.
Image: Bodleian Library, MS Douce 204, f. 37. By permission of the Bodleian
    Library, University of Oxford.

*How to Attack an Enemy Ship*, 1441:

Mariano di Jacopo Taccola, *De ingeneis: Liber primus leonis, liber secundus draconis,
    addenda*; Books I and II, On Engines, and Addenda, ed. and trans. Giustina
    Scaglia, Frank D. Prager, and Ulrich Montag, 2 vols. (Wiesbaden, 1984), 46.
    (Translation slightly adapted.)
The technological treatises of the Sienese engineer Mariano Taccola exist only in
    manuscript versions.
Image: British Library, Royal MS 14 E IV, f. 276r. © The British Library Board.

*How to Attract a Lover*, 1699:

*Aristotle's Legacy: or, His Golden Cabinet of Secrets Opened* (London, 1699), 18.
One of many texts which sought legitimacy by name-dropping the philosopher,
    this fortune-telling manual was first printed around 1690.
Image: *The Jovial Marriner* (1670-82[?]). Courtesy of the Beinecke Rare Book and
    Manuscript Library, Yale University.

*How to Avoid an Acquaintance*, 1881:

John H. Young, *Our Deportment, Or the Manners, Conduct and Dress of the Most
    Refined Society* (Detroit, 1881), 48.

Image: *Routledges Ball Room Guide* (1866?). Courtesy of the George Peabody Library, The Sheridan Libraries, Johns Hopkins University.

## How to *Avoid the Plague,* 1579:

Thomas Lupton, *A Thousand Notable Things, of Sundry Sortes* (London, 1579), 57.
Lupton's miscellaneous compendium of remarkable anecdotes and thrifty tips, first published in 1579, was so popular that it continued to be published into the nineteenth century.
Image: Hans Holbein, *Simolachri: Historie e figure de la morte* (1549). Courtesy of the George Peabody Library, The Sheridan Libraries, Johns Hopkins University.

## How to *Avoid Pregnancy,* twelfth century:

*The Trotula: A Medieval Compendium of Women's Medicine,* ed. and trans. Monica H. Green (Philadelphia, 2001), 97–9.
The collection of women's medical knowledge known as the *Trotula* circulated in different versions in the Middle Ages; though a kernel of the text is associated with the female physician Trota of Salerno, the *Trotula* consists of three separate texts, which all came to be associated with a mythical figure named Trotula.
Image: British Library, Sloane MS 2435, f. 9v. © The British Library Board.

## How to *Be a Baroness,* 1404:

Christine de Pizan, *A Medieval Woman's Mirror of Honor. The Treasury of the City of Ladies,* trans. Charity Cannon Willard, ed. Madeleine Pelner Cosman (New York, 1989), 168–70.
Christine de Pizan followed her famous *Livre de la Cité des Dames (Book of the City of Ladies)* with this instructional compendium for women, *Le Trésor de la Cité des Dames,* also in Middle French.
Image: Walters Art Museum, W.141, f. 28v. © Walters Art Museum, used under a Creative Commons Attribution-ShareAlike 3.0 license.

## How to *Be a Head Chef,* 1473:

Olivier de la Marche, *Mémoires,* trans. Terence Scully, in Scully, *Early French Cookery: Sources, History, Original Recipes and Modern Adaptations* (Ann Arbor, 1995), 46.
The *Mémoires* of Olivier de la Marche, courtier, poet, and *maître d'hôtel* to Charles the Bold of Burgundy, cover the second half of the fifteenth century.
Image: Hans Sachs, *Eygentliche Beschreibung aller Stände auff Erden* (1568). Courtesy of the Beinecke Rare Book and Manuscript Library, Yale University.

*How to Behave at School, 1595:*

William Fiston, *The Schoole of Good Manners: Or, a New Schoole of Vertue* (London, 1595), C5r–v.

An early English imitaton of Erasmus's *De civilitate*, based on a French paraphrase.

Image: Francesco Petrarca, *De rebus memorandis*, trans. Stefan Vigilius (1566). Courtesy of the George Peabody Library, The Sheridan Libraries, Johns Hopkins University.

*How to Belch Politely, 1640:*

Lucas Gracián Dantisco, *Galateo Espagnol, or The Spanish Gallant*, trans. W[illiam] S[tyle] (London, 1640), 9.

Dantisco's Spanish adaptation of the *Galateo* was published in the 1590s and translated into English in 1640.

Image: David Deuchar, Man at a Table. Courtesy of the Wellcome Library, London.

*How to Blow Your Nose, 1616:*

Thomas Gainsford, *The Rich Cabinet… Whereunto is Annexed the Epitome of Good Manners, Extracted from Mr. Iohn de la Casa, Arch-bishop of Beneventa* (London, 1616), Z1r–v.

An English adaptation of Giovanni della Casa's *Galateo*.

Image: Hendrick Goltzius, *Portrait of a Man* (1607). The J. Paul Getty Museum. Image courtesy of the Getty's Open Content Program.

*How to Breed Horses, 1620:*

Nicholas Morgan, *The Horse-mans Honour, or, The Beautie of Horsemanship* (London, 1620), 108–9.

Image: "A Dappled Gray Stallion Tethered in a Landscape" (c. 1584·7). The J. Paul Getty Museum. Image courtesy of the Getty's Open Content Program.

*How to Caper in Water, 1595:*

Everard Digby, *De arte natandi*, trans. Christopher Middleton, *A Short Introduction for to Learne to Swimme* (London, 1595), K2v.

Digby's Latin swimming manual was published in 1587.

Image: Everard Digby, *De arte natandi* (1587). Courtesy of the John Work Garrett Library, The Sheridan Libraries, Johns Hopkins University.

*How to Care for a Newborn, 1256:*

Aldobrandino of Siena, *Le régime du corps de Maître Aldebrandin de Sienne*, trans. Faith Wallis, in *Medieval Medicine: A Reader* (Toronto, 2010), 495–6.

Aldobrandino compiled his dietetic text in French for Countess Beatrice of Savoy, drawing on influential medical authors like Avicenna and Rhazes.
Image: Walters Art Museum, W.106, f. 18v. © Walters Art Museum, used under a Creative Commons Attribution·ShareAlike 3.0 license.

### *How to Care for Your Cat, c. 1260:*

Albertus Magnus, *De animalibus*, trans. Kenneth F. Kitchell Jr. and Irven Michael Resnick, *On Animals: A Medieval Summa Zoologica*, 2 vols. (Baltimore, 1999), 1523.
St. Albert, German Dominican philosopher, theologian, and bishop, came to be known as the "universal doctor" thanks to the breadth of his intellectual inquiries.
Image: Bibliothèque nationale de France, NAL 3134, f. 80r.

### *How to Care for Your Dog, c. 1393:*

*Le Ménagier de Paris*, trans. Gina L. Greco and Christine M. Rose, *The Good Wife's Guide: A Medieval Household Book* (Ithaca, NY, 2009), 234.
*Le Ménagier de Paris*, composed in French in the voice of a husband instructing his young wife, contains tips on household management, along with 380 recipes.
Image: Morgan Library, MS M.1044, f. 44v. Gaston Phebus, *Livre de la chasse*, c. 1406–7. Bequest of Clara S. Peck, 1983. The Pierpont Morgan Library, New York/Art Resource, NY.

### *How to Care for Your Lawn, c. 1260:*

Albertus Magnus, *De vegetabilibus libri VII*, trans. Christopher Thacker, *The History of Gardens* (London, 1979), 84.
Image: The J. Paul Getty Museum, MS Ludwig IX 8, f. 6r. Image courtesy of the Getty's Open Content Program.

### *How to Care for Your Lute, 1676:*

Thomas Mace, *Musick's Monument; or, a Remembrancer of the Best Practical Musick* (London, 1676), 62; 64.
Mace's handbook contains introductions to both the lute and the viol.
Image: Hans Sachs, *Eygentliche Beschreibung aller Stände auff Erden* (1568). Courtesy of the Beinecke Rare Book and Manuscript Library, Yale University.

### *How to Catch Flies, c. 1393:*

*Le Ménagier de Paris*, trans. Greco and Rose, 140.
See *How to Care for Your Dog, c. 1393.*
Image: St. Gallen, Kantonsbibliothek, Vadianische Sammlung, Ms. 343c, f. 72r.

*How to Catch a Ray*, 1658:

Giambattista della Porta, *Natural Magick: in XX Bookes by John Baptista Porta, a Neopolitaine* (London, 1658), 331-2.

Della Porta's *Magia naturalis*, first published in 1558, explains the miraculous phenomena of the natural world; this is the first English edition.

Image: Ulisse Aldrovandi, *De piscibus* (1638). Courtesy of the John Work Garrett Library, The Sheridan Libraries, Johns Hopkins University.

*How to Change a Diaper*, 1612:

Jacques Guillemeau, *Child-birth or, the Happy Deliuerie of Women* (London, 1612), 21.

Image: Francesco Petrarca, *De rebus memorandis*, trans. Stefan Vigilius (1566). Courtesy of the George Peabody Library, The Sheridan Libraries, Johns Hopkins University.

*How to Charm a Man*, 1896:

*The Ladies' Book of Useful Information. Compiled from Many Sources* (London, ON, 1896), 72.

Image: *La légende de Béguinette* (1903). Courtesy of the Milton S. Eisenhower Library, The Sheridan Libraries, Johns Hopkins University.

*How to Chat with a Woman*, c. 1180s:

Andreas Capellanus, *De amore*, ed. and trans. P. G. Walsh, *On Love* (London, 1982), 47.

*De amore* (*On Love*) is the classic medieval explanation of the phenomenon of "courtly love."

Image: British Library, Royal MS 14 E III, f. 146r. © The British Library Board.

*How to Choose a Cook*, 1474:

Bartolomeo Platina, *De honesta voluptate et valetudine*, trans. Mary Ella Milham, Platina, *On Right Pleasure and Good Health: A Critical Edition and Translation of De honesta voluptate et valetudine* (Tempe, AZ, 1998), 119.

Bartolomeo Sacchi (known as Platina after his birthplace) began his career as a mercenary soldier and ended it as head librarian of the Vatican. He is the author of the first printed cookbook.

Image: Bartolomeo Scappi, *Opera* (1570). Courtesy of the Milton S. Eisenhower Library, The Sheridan Libraries, Johns Hopkins University.

*How to Clean Your Teeth*, 1561:

Hieronymus Brunschwig, *A Most Excellent and Perfecte Homish Apothecarye or Homely Physik Book*, trans. John Hollybush [?](London, 1561), 18.

The first English translation of Hieronymus Brunschwig's *Thesaurus pauperum: Hauß Apotek*, first published in 1507.

Image: Edward Topsell, *The Historie of Foure-Footed Beastes* (1675). Courtesy of the George Peabody Library, The Sheridan Libraries, Johns Hopkins University.

## *How to Clear Your Head*, 1623:

Tobias Venner, *Via recta ad vitam longam, pars secunda* (London, 1623), 27.

Image: Magnus Hundt, *Antropologium de hominis dignitate* (1501). Courtesy of the Wellcome Library, London.

## *How to Compliment a Lady*, 1663:

John Gough, *The Academy of Complements* (London, 1663), 92–6.

First published in 1639.

Image: *Advice to the Ladies of London* (1686–8?). Courtesy of the Beinecke Rare Book and Manuscript Library, Yale University.

## *How to Converse*, 1646:

Francis Hawkins, *Youths Behaviour, or, Decency in Conversation Amongst Men* (London, 1646), 6.

*Youths Behaviour*, first published around 1640, is a translation of a French work, *Bienséance de la conversation entre les hommes* (1617), itself based on the *Galateo*.

Image: Desiderius Erasmus, *Moriæ encomium*, trans. White Kennett (1709). Courtesy of the George Peabody Library, The Sheridan Libraries, Johns Hopkins University.

## *How to Cook a Porcupine*, 1570:

Bartolomeo Scappi, *Opera*, trans. Terence Scully, *The Opera of Bartolomeo Scappi (1570): L'arte et Prudenza d'un Maestro Cuoco* (Toronto, 2008), 179.

Bartolomeo Scappi was private chef to several popes and the author, in 1570, of one of the most influential cookbooks of Renaissance Italy.

Image: Conrad Gesner, *Historiae animalium* (1551). Courtesy of the George Peabody Library, The Sheridan Libraries, Johns Hopkins University.

## *How to Cure Gas*, 1685:

Nicolas Lemery, *Modern Curiosities of Art and Nature* (London, 1685), 59–60.

First published in French in 1684.

Image: Izaak Walton, *The Compleat Angler* (1665). Courtesy of the George Peabody Library, The Sheridan Libraries, Johns Hopkins University.

## How to Cure Head Congestion, 1596:

A. T., *A Rich Store-House or Treasury for the Diseased* (London, 1596), 48.

Image: Francesco Petrarca, *De rebus memorandis*, trans. Stefan Vigilius (1566). Courtesy of the George Peabody Library, The Sheridan Libraries, Johns Hopkins University.

## How to Cure a Headache, ninth century:

Pseudo-Pliny, trans. H. S. Versnel, "The Poetics of the Magical Charm: An Essay on the Power of Words," in Paul Mirecki and Marvin Meyer, eds., *Magic and Ritual in the Ancient World* (Leiden, 2002), 119–20.

This advice appears in a ninth-century manuscript (St. Gallen, Stiftsbibliothek Cod. Sang. 751) as an addition to a late antique medical text.

Image: Burgerbibliothek Bern, Cod. 264, p. 79.

## How to Cure a Headache, 1561:

Hieronymus Brunschwig, *A Most Excellent and Perfecte Homish Apothecarye or Homely Physik Book*, trans. Hollybush, 4.

See *How to Clean Your Teeth, 1561.*

Image: Hans Sachs, *Eygentliche Beschreibung aller Stände auff Erden* (1568). Courtesy of the Beinecke Rare Book and Manuscript Library, Yale University.

## How to Cure Insomnia, 1597:

William Langham, *The Garden of Health* (London, 1597), 356–7.

Image: Francesco Petrarca, *De rebus memorandis*, trans. Stefan Vigilius (1566). Courtesy of the George Peabody Library, The Sheridan Libraries, Johns Hopkins University.

## How to Cure Laryngitis, 1579:

Thomas Lupton, *A Thousand Notable Things*, 154–5.

See *How to Avoid the Plague, 1579.*

Image: Francesco Maria Guazzo, *Compendium maleficarum* (1626). Courtesy of the George Peabody Library, The Sheridan Libraries, Johns Hopkins University.

## How to Cure Lovesickness, eleventh century:

Constantinus Africanus, *Viaticum*, ed. and trans. Mary Frances Wack, *Lovesickness in the Middle Ages: The Viaticum and Its Commentaries* (Philadelphia, 1990), 191.

"Constantine the African" was born in North Africa and became a monk at Monte Cassino in southern Italy, where he translated important Arabic medical texts into Latin.

Image: Bodleian Library, MS Rawl. Q. b. 5, f. 162r. By permission of the Bodleian Library, University of Oxford.

## How to Cure Nausea, 1693:

Robert Boyle, *Medicinal Experiments, or, a Collection of Choice and Safe Remedies* (London, 1693), 175.

Boyle's collection was first printed in 1688.

Image: P. Boone, *Allegories of the Senses* (1561). Courtesy of the Wellcome Library, London.

## How to Cure a Nosebleed, 1673:

William Sermon, *A Friend to the Sick: or, the Honest English Mans Preservation* (London, 1673), 80.

Image: *Ortus sanitatis* (1497). Courtesy of the Harvey Cushing/John Hay Whitney Medical Library, Yale University.

## How to Cure Pimples, 1665:

Thomas Jeamson, *Artificiall Embellishments, or Arts Best Directions* (London, 1665), 71–4.

Image: John Bulwer, *Anthropometamorphosis* (1653). Courtesy of the George Peabody Library, The Sheridan Libraries, Johns Hopkins University.

## How to Cure Seasickness, 1695:

Maximilien Misson, *A New Voyage to Italy* (London, 1695), II.335.

Misson published accounts of several voyages, among them the *Nouveau voyage d'Italie* of 1691.

Image: Francesco Petrarca, *De rebus memorandis*, trans. Stefan Vigilius (1566). Courtesy of the George Peabody Library, The Sheridan Libraries, Johns Hopkins University.

## How to Cure a Sore Throat, 1685:

Nicolas Lemery, *Modern Curiosities of Art and Nature*, 72.

See *How to Cure Gas, 1685.*

Image: Jean Baudoin, *Les fables d'Esope* (1649). Courtesy of the George Peabody Library, The Sheridan Libraries, Johns Hopkins University.

## How to Cure Soreness, 1835:

Charles Random de Berenger, *Helps and Hints How to Protect Life and Property* (London, 1835), 110.

Image: William Heath, "Do you care to have your bed warm'd sir?" (1828?)
Courtesy of the Lewis Walpole Library, Yale University.

### How to Cure a Toothache, 1779:

*The London Practice of Physic*, 4th ed. (Dublin, 1779), 154.
The first edition was published in 1769.
Image: Thomas Rowlandson, "Transplanting of Teeth" (1790). Courtesy of the
Wellcome Library, London.

### How to Dance, c. 1455:

Domenico da Piacenza, *De arte saltandi*, ed. and trans. A. William Smith, *Fifteenth-Century Dance and Music: Treatises and Music* (Hillsdale, NY, 1995), 13.
(Translation slightly adapted.)
The Italian dancing treatise of Domenico da Piacenza, dance master in Ferrara, is
the earliest such text to survive.
Image: Österreichische Nationalbibliothek, Cod. Vindob. series nova 2644, f. 104r.

### How to Decorate the Table, 1474:

Bartolomeo Platina, *De honesta voluptate et valetudine*, trans. Milham, 119.
See *How to Choose a Cook, 1474.*
Image: Theodor Graminaeus, *Beschreibung derer Fürstlicher Güligscher &c. Hochzeit*
(1587). The J. Paul Getty Museum. Courtesy of the Getty's Open Content
Program.

### How to Defend Yourself from Basil, 1579:

Thomas Lupton, *A Thousand Notable Things*, 10.
See *How to Avoid the Plague, 1579.*
Image: John Gerard, *The Herball or Generall Historie of Plantes* (1633). Courtesy
of the George Peabody Library, The Sheridan Libraries, Johns Hopkins
University.

### How to Dress for Bathing, 1881:

John H. Young, *Our Deportment*, 334.
See *How to Avoid an Acquaintance, 1881.*
Image: *The Daily Graphic* (June 1879). Courtesy of the George Peabody Library,
The Sheridan Libraries, Johns Hopkins University.

### How to Dress for Cycling, 1896:

John Wesley Hanson, *Etiquette and Bicycling, for* 1896 (Chicago, 1896), 366.

Image: *Harper's Bazaar* 29, no. 11 (March 14, 1896). Courtesy of the George Peabody Library, The Sheridan Libraries, Johns Hopkins University.

## How to Dress for Dancing, 1538:

Antonius Arena, *Leges dansandi.* In *Antonius Arena, Provincialis de bragardissima villa de Soleriis, ad suos compagnones studiantes…* (Lyon, 1538), ed. and trans. John Guthrie and Marino Zorzi, "Rules of Dancing," *Dance Research* 4, no. 2 (1986): 3–53, at 28.

Antonius Arena (Antoine Arène) first published his macaronic *Leges dansandi* (*Dancing Rules*) in 1529 appended to his work *Ad suos compagnones studiantes.* The earthy advice on dance etiquette first appeared in subsequent editions in 1529 and 1531.

Image: Cesare Negri, *Nuove inventioni di balli* (1604). Courtesy of the Beinecke Rare Book and Manuscript Library, Yale University.

## How to Dress to Impress, 1632:

Nicolas Faret, *The Honest Man: or, the Art to Please in Court*, trans. E. G. (London, 1632), 357–9.

A translation of Faret's *L'Honneste-Homme* (1630).

Image: Cesare Ripa, *Iconologia* (1644). Courtesy of the Beinecke Rare Book and Manuscript Library, Yale University.

## How to Dress Your Child, c. 1200:

Daniel of Beccles, *Urbanus magnus*, ed. Josiah Gilbart Smyly (Dublin, 1939), 80. (My translation.)

*Urbanus magnus* is a lengthy Latin poem of advice for a broad range of medieval situations.

Image: Cesare Ripa, *Iconologia* (1644). Courtesy of the Beinecke Rare Book and Manuscript Library, Yale University.

## How to Drink Beer, 1623:

Tobias Venner, *Via recta ad vitam longam*, 44–6.

See *How to Clear Your Head, 1623.*

Image: Giambattista della Porta, *De humana physiognomia* (1602). Courtesy of the Harvey Cushing/John Hay Whitney Medical Library, Yale University.

## How to Dye Your Hair Green, 1563:

Alessio Piemontese [Girolamo Ruscelli?], *The Second Part of the Secretes of Maister Alexis of Piemont*, trans. William Ward (London, 1563), 17.

The collection of secrets of "Alessio Piemontese" was the prototype and most
popular example of its genre; published in 1555, it saw seventy editions in eight
languages by 1600.

Image: John Bulwer, *Anthropometamorphosis* (1653). Courtesy of the George
Peabody Library, The Sheridan Libraries, Johns Hopkins University.

## How to Eat Politely, 1646:

Francis Hawkins, *Youths Behaviour*, 34.

See *How to Converse, 1646.*

Image: Francesco Petrarca, *De rebus memorandis*, trans. Stefan Vigilius (1566).
Courtesy of the George Peabody Library, The Sheridan Libraries, Johns
Hopkins University.

## How to Eat Soup, 1595:

William Fiston, *The Schoole of Good Manners*, Dıv.

See *How to Behave in School, 1595.*

Image: Francesco Petrarca, *De rebus memorandis*, trans. Stefan Vigilius (1566).
Courtesy of the George Peabody Library, The Sheridan Libraries, Johns
Hopkins University.

## How to Escape from Prison, 1642:

Mario Bettinus, *Apiaria universae philosophiae mathematicae* (Bologna, 1642), 30.

Image: Mario Bettinus, *Apiaria universae philosophiae mathematicae* (1642). Courtesy
of the George Peabody Library, The Sheridan Libraries, Johns Hopkins
University.

## How to Exercise, 1623:

Tobias Venner, *Via recta ad vitam longam*, 21–2.

See *How to Clear Your Head, 1623.*

Image: Isaac Fuller, *Iconologia* (1709). Courtesy of the Wellcome Library, London.

## How to Fart, 1530:

Desiderius Erasmus, *De civilitate morum puerilium libellum* (Basel, 1530), 17–8. (My
translation.)

Erasmus's *De civilitate morum puerilium libellum (Handbook of Good Manners for
Boys)*, first published in 1530, is one of the foundational European texts on
civility.

Image: Cesare Negri, *Nuove inventioni di balli* (1604). Courtesy of the Beinecke
Rare Book and Manuscript Library, Yale University.

### How to Fatten Up, 1665:

Thomas Jeamson, *Artificiall Embellishments*, 65–7.
See *How to Cure Pimples, 1665.*
Image: John Bulwer, *Anthropometamorphosis* (1653). Courtesy of the George
   Peabody Library, The Sheridan Libraries, Johns Hopkins University.

### How to Feed Your Child, 1692:

John Locke, *Some Thoughts Concerning Education*, ed. Ruth W. Grant and Nathan
   Tarcov (Indianapolis, 1996), 18.
Locke's *Thoughts Concerning Education* originated as advice to a friend on child-rearing.
Image: Heinrich von Louffenberg, *Artzneybuch* (1546). Courtesy of the Wellcome
   Library, London.

### How to Fold Fabulous Napkins, 1629:

*Li tre trattati di messer Mattia Giegher Bavaro di Mosburc* (Padua, 1629), 10–12.
*Li tre trattati* of the German Mattia Giegher (Matthias Jäger), working in Padua,
   includes the first comprehensive printed instructions in the art of folding
   table linens.
Image: *Li tre trattati* (1629). The J. Paul Getty Museum. Image courtesy of the
   Getty's Open Content Program.

### How to Garden with Lobsters, 1777:

*The Complete Vermin-Killer: A Valuable and Useful Companion for Families, in Town
   and Country*, 4th ed. (London, 1777), 66.
Image: Joannes Jonstonus, *Historiæ naturalis de piscibus et cetis* (1649). Courtesy of the
   George Peabody Library, The Sheridan Libraries, Johns Hopkins University.

### How to Get Pregnant, 1671:

William Sermon, *The Ladies Companion, or the English Midwife* (London, 1671), 13.
Image: Cesare Ripa, *Iconologia* (1644). Courtesy of the Beinecke Rare Book and
   Manuscript Library, Yale University.

### How to Get Rich, 1556:

Georgius Agricola, *De re metallica*, trans. Herbert Clark Hoover and Lou Henry
   Hoover, *De re metallica libri XII* (London, 1912), xxv; 6.
*De re metallica (On Metals)* of the German metallurgist Georg Bauer (Georgius
   Agricola) remained influential after its publication in 1556; the first English
   translation was published in 1912 by Lou Henry Hoover and Herbert Hoover,
   future U.S. president.

Image: Francesco Petrarca, *De rebus memorandis*, trans. Stefan Vigilius (1566). Courtesy of the George Peabody Library, The Sheridan Libraries, Johns Hopkins University.

### *How to Get Rid of a Contentious Man*, 1727:

Thomas Parkyns, *Progymnasmata: The inn-play: or, Cornish-hugg wrestler*, 3rd ed. (London, 1727), 58.

Image: Thomas Parkyns, *Progymnasmata* (1727). Courtesy of the George Peabody Library, The Sheridan Libraries, Johns Hopkins University.

### *How to Get Rid of Mosquitoes*, c. 1260:

Albertus Magnus, *De animalibus*, trans. Kitchell and Resnick, 1477.

See *How to Care for Your Cat, c. 1260.*

Image: The J. Paul Getty Museum, MS Ludwig XV 3, f. 99r. Image courtesy of the Getty's Open Content Program.

### *How to Give Birth*, c. 1450:

Michele Savonarola, *Ad mulieres ferrarienses de regimine pregnantium et noviter natorum usque ad septennium*, ed. Luigi Belloni, *Il trattato ginecologico-pediatrico in volgare* (Milan, 1952), 121. (My translation.)

Michele Savonarola, grandfather of the visionary friar Girolamo Savonarola, was a celebrated physician and author of numerous medical treatises, including this book of medical advice for the women of Ferrara.

Image: British Library, Royal MS 15 E VI, f. 273r. © The British Library Board.

### *How to Give Someone Gas*, 1660:

Johann Jacob Wecker, *Eighteen Books of the Secrets of Art & Nature* (London, 1660), 21–2.

An English translation of Wecker's Latin compendium, *De secretis libri XVIII*, published in 1582.

Image: Hugh Plat, *The Jewel House of Art and Nature* (1653). Courtesy of the George Peabody Library, The Sheridan Libraries, Johns Hopkins University.

### *How to Groom Your Eyebrows*, 1563:

Alessio Piemontese [Girolamo Ruscelli?], *The Second Part of the Secretes of Maister Alexis of Piemont*, trans. Ward, 10.

See *How to Dye Your Hair Green, 1563.*

Image: John Bulwer, *Anthropometamorphosis* (1653). Courtesy of the George Peabody Library, The Sheridan Libraries, Johns Hopkins University.

## How to Grow a Beard, 1544:

*Traicté nouveau, intitulé, Bastiment des receptes: nouvellement traduict de Italien en langue Françoyse* (Poitiers, 1544), B6v. (My translation.)

A French translation of the 1529 Italian household manual *Dificio di Recetti*.

Image: John Bulwer, *Anthropometamorphosis* (1653). Courtesy of the George Peabody Library, The Sheridan Libraries, Johns Hopkins University.

## How to Handle Books, 1345:

Richard de Bury, *Philobiblon*, trans. E. C. Thomas (London, 1903), 105.

English bishop Richard de Bury was an early book collector whose *Philobiblon* (*Love of Books*) discusses the collection, care, and defense of books.

Image: Beinecke Library, Marston MS 67, f. 66r. Courtesy of the Beinecke Rare Book and Manuscript Library, Yale University.

## How to Harvest the Mandrake, twelfth century:

*Apuleii liber de medicaminibus herbarum*, ed. and trans. George C. Druce, "The Elephant in Medieval Legend and Art," *Journal of the Royal Archaeological Institute* 76 (1919), 46.

Image: Wellcome MS 573, f. 53v. Courtesy of the Wellcome Library, London.

## How to Harvest Melons, 1691:

Nicolas de Bonnefons, *The French Gardiner*, trans. John Evelyn. 4th ed. (London, 1691), 108.

Evelyn's translation of this popular French gardening manual was first published in 1658 (the original appeared in 1651).

Image: Elizabeth Blackwell, *Herbarium Blackwellianum* (1757). Courtesy of the Beinecke Rare Book and Manuscript Library, Yale University.

## How to Have a Beautiful Child, 1697:

*Aristotle's Master-piece Compleated* (London, 1697), 16–17.

One of a number of texts which sought to legitimize their endeavors by mentioning Aristotle, this manual deals with gynecology and reproduction.

Image: Giambattista della Porta, *De humana physiognomia* (1602). Courtesy of the Harvey Cushing/John Hay Whitney Medical Library, Yale University.

## How to Have a Performing Dog, c. 1260:

Albertus Magnus, *De animalibus*, trans. Kitchell and Resnick, 1460.

See *How to Care for Your Cat, c. 1260.*

Image: Walters Art Museum, W.102, f. 75v. © Walters Art Museum, used under a
Creative Commons Attribution-ShareAlike 3.0 license.

### *How to Heal All Wounds*, 1686:

Hannah Woolley, *The Accomplish'd Ladies Delight in Preserving, Physick, Beautifying, and Cookery* (London, 1686), 86.
First published in 1685.
Image: Hans von Gersdorff, *Feldtbuch der Wundartzney* (1530). Courtesy of the Wellcome Library, London.

### *How to Impress Girls at a Dance*, 1538:

Antonius Arena, *Leges dansandi*, trans. Guthrie and Zorzi, 33–5. Translation slightly adapted.
See *How to Dress for Dancing, 1538.*
Image: Fabritio Caroso, *Il ballarino* (1581). Courtesy of the Beinecke Rare Book and Manuscript Library, Yale University.

### *How to Improve Your Memory*, 1563:

Alessio Piemontese [Girolamo Ruscelli?], *The Second Part of the Secretes of Maister Alexis of Piemont*, trans. Ward, 8–9.
See *How to Dye Your Hair Green, 1563.*
Image: Edward Topsell, *The Historie of Foure-Footed Beastes* (1675). Courtesy of the George Peabody Library, The Sheridan Libraries, Johns Hopkins University.

### *How to Increase Lust*, eleventh century:

Constantinus Africanus, *Constantini Liber de coitu*, trans. Faith Wallis, *Medieval Medicine: A Reader* (Toronto, 2010), 520–22.
See *How to Cure Lovesickness, eleventh century.*
Image: The J. Paul Getty Museum, MS 100, f. 58r. Image courtesy of the Getty's Open Content Program.

### *How to Interpret Dreams*, c. 1100:

Germanus, *Oneirocriticon*, trans. Steven M. Oberhelman, *Dreambooks in Byzantium: Six Oneirocritica in Translation, with Commentary* (Aldershot, 2008), 153–66.
The *Oneirocriticon* of Germanus, one in a long tradition of dream-interpretation manuals, is a Byzantine text from sometime between 900 and 1300.

Image: British Library, Harley MS 4867, f. 74v. © The British Library Board.

### How to Interview People Abroad, 1789:

Leopold Berchtold, *An Essay to Direct and Extend the Inquiries of Patriotic Travellers* (London, 1789), 99; 187; 260; 320; 428.

Austrian traveler Leopold Berchtold offers both practical advice and an enormous collection of precise questions for the curious traveler.

Image: James Bretherton, "A Tour to Foreign Parts" (1778). Courtesy of the Lewis Walpole Library, Yale University.

### How to Keep Your Cat, c. 1470:

*The Distaff Gospels: A First Modern Edition of* Les Évangiles des Quenouilles, ed. and trans. Madeleine Jeay and Kathleen Garay (Peterborough, ON, and Orchard Park, NY, 2006), 237–9.

*Les Evangiles des Quenouilles* is a collection of late medieval women's popular beliefs that uses women's gatherings as a narrative framework.

Image: Beinecke Library, MS 404, f. 148r. Courtesy of the Beinecke Rare Book and Manuscript Library, Yale University.

### How to Keep Your Hands Warm, 1579:

Thomas Lupton, *A Thousand Notable Things*, 61.

See *How to Avoid the Plague, 1579.*

Image: Walters Art Museum, W.425, f. 12r. © Walters Art Museum, used under a Creative Commons Attribution-ShareAlike 3.0 license.

### How to Kill Bedbugs, 1777:

*The Complete Vermin-Killer*, 3–4.

See *How to Garden with Lobsters, 1777.*

Image: John Southall, *A Treatise of Buggs* (1730). Courtesy of the Beinecke Rare Book and Manuscript Library, Yale University.

### How to Kill Fleas, 1688:

R. W., *A Necessary Family-Book* (London, 1688), 33.

Image: Robert Hooke, *Micrographia* (1665). Courtesy of the Milton S. Eisenhower Library, The Sheridan Libraries, Johns Hopkins University.

### How to Kill Snakes, 1688:

R. W., *A Necessary Family-Book*, 18.

See *How to Kill Fleas, 1688.*

Image: Jean Baudoin, *Les fables d'Esope* (1649). Courtesy of the George Peabody Library, The Sheridan Libraries, Johns Hopkins University.

## *How to Kiss,* 1777:

*A Dictionary of Love, with Notes* (London, 1777), s.v. "Kiss."

Image: "The Honey-moon" (1777). Courtesy of the Lewis Walpole Library, Yale University.

## *How to Know If Death Is Imminent, fifth century:*

Pseudo-Hippocrates, *Capsula eburnea,* trans. Faith Wallis, *Medieval Medicine: A Reader* (Toronto, 2010), 44.

The *Capsula eburnea (Ivory Casket),* also known as *Prognostica,* appears to be a fifth- or sixth-century Latin version of a late Greek text on prognostications.

Image: Österreichische Nationalbibliothek, Cod. Med. Graec. 1, f. 312r.

## *How to Know If You're Pregnant,* 1685:

Nicolas Lemery, *Modern Curiosities of Art and Nature,* 70.

See *How to Cure Gas, 1685.*

Image: Ulisse Aldrovandi, *Monstrorum historia* (1642). Courtesy of the George Peabody Library, The Sheridan Libraries, Johns Hopkins University.

## *How to Know the Moon's Phase,* 1658:

John White, *A Rich Cabinet, with Variety of Inventions* (London, 1658), 33.

White's *Rich Cabinet,* the first in a series of collections of conceits, was first published in 1651.

Image: Edward Topsell, *The Historie of Foure-Footed Beastes* (1675). Courtesy of the George Peabody Library, The Sheridan Libraries, Johns Hopkins University.

## *How to Leave a Party,* c. 1200:

Daniel of Beccles, *Urbanus magnus,* 51. (My translation.)

See *How to Dress Your Child, c. 1200.*

Image: The J. Paul Getty Museum, MS Ludwig XIV 6, f. 27r. Image courtesy of the Getty's Open Content Program.

## *How to Light a Fire,* 1612:

*The Booke of Pretty Conceits,* A2r.

See *How to Sober Up, 1612.*

Image: Francesco Maria Guazzo, *Compendium maleficarum* (1626). Courtesy of the George Peabody Library, The Sheridan Libraries, Johns Hopkins University.

*How to Live, c. 1200:*

Daniel of Beccles, *Urbanus magnus*, 92. (My translation.)

See *How to Dress Your Child, c. 1200.*

Image: Walters Art Museum, W.760, f. 173r. © Walters Art Museum, used under a
  Creative Commons Attribution-ShareAlike 3.0 license.

*How to Look Good on a Budget, c. 1280:*

Amanieu de Sescás, *Enssenhamen de l'escudier*, trans. Mark. D. Johnston, "The
  Occitan *Enssenhamen de l'escudier* and *Essenhamen de la donzela* of Amanieu de
  Sescás," in Mark D. Johnston, ed., *Medieval Conduct Literature: An Anthology
  of Vernacular Guides to Behaviour for Youths, with English Translations* (Toronto,
  2009), 31–2.

Little is known about Amanieu de Sescás, who composed two poetic advice
  manuals, *Enssenhamen de l'escudier* (*Instruction for a Squire*) and *Essenhamen de la
  donzela* (*Instruction for a Young Lady*), in Old Occitan.

Image: Österreichische Nationalbibliothek, Cod. Vindob. series nova 2644, f. 105r.

*How to Look Good While Dancing, 1538:*

Antonius Arena, *Leges dansandi*. (My translation.)

See *How to Dress for Dancing, 1538.*

Image: Cesare Negri, *Nuove inventioni di balli* (1604). Courtesy of the Beinecke
  Rare Book and Manuscript Library, Yale University.

*How to Make Bird Missiles, thirteenth century:*

Marcus Graecus, *Liber ignium ad comburendos hostes*, ed. and trans. J. R. Partington,
  *A History of Greek Fire and Gunpowder* (Baltimore, 1960), 46.

The *Liber ignium ad comburendos hostes* (*Book of Fires for Burning Enemies*) seems to
  have originated around the thirteenth century.

Image: British Library, Additional MS 42130, f. 171r. © The British Library Board.

*How to Make a Cheesy Omelet, c. 1393:*

*Le Ménagier de Paris*, trans. Greco and Rose, 310–11.

See *How to Care for Your Dog, c. 1393.*

Image: Österreichische Nationalbibliothek, Cod. Vindob. series nova 2644, f. 65v.

*How to Make Chocolate, 1685:*

Philippe Sylvestre Dufour, *The Manner of Making Coffee, Tea and Chocolate*, trans.
  John Chamberlayn (London, 1685), 72.

Image: Jean de Laet, *Histoire du nouveau monde* (1640). Courtesy of the Beinecke Rare Book and Manuscript Library, Yale University.

### How to Make a Christmas Pie, 1774:

Hannah Glasse, *The Art of Cookery Made Plain and Easy* (London, 1774), 139–40. The first edition was published in 1747.
Image: Charles Elmé Francatelli, *The Modern Cook* (1846). Courtesy of the Yale University Libraries.

### How to Make Cock Ale, 1697:

*A New Book of Knowledge* (London, 1697), 3.
Image: Hans Sachs, *Eygentliche Beschreibung aller Stände auff Erden* (1568). Courtesy of the Beinecke Rare Book and Manuscript Library, Yale University.

### How to Make Coffee, 1685:

Philippe Sylvestre Dufour, *The Manner of Making Coffee, Tea and Chocolate*, trans. Chamberlayn, 8–10.
See *How to Make Chocolate, 1685.*
Image: Philippe Sylvestre Dufour, *The Manner of Making Coffee, Tea and Chocolate* (1685). Courtesy of the Beinecke Rare Book and Manuscript Library, Yale University.

### How to Make a Cooked Bird Sing, c. 1450:

*The Vivendier: A Critical Edition with English Translation*, ed. and trans. Terence Scully (Devon, 1997), 83.
*The Vivendier* is a French recipe collection surviving in a single manuscript.
Image: British Library, Additional MS 42130, f. 207v. © The British Library Board.

### How to Make Dinner Conversation, 1576:

Thomas Twyne, *The Schoolemaster, or Teacher of Table Philosophie* (London, 1576). An adaptation of a medieval dietary manual, the *Mensa philosophica.*
Image: Girolamo Mercuriale, *De arte gymnastica* (1601). Courtesy of the George Peabody Library, The Sheridan Libraries, Johns Hopkins University.

### How to Make a Dragon out of Fireworks, 1658:

John White, *A Rich Cabinet*, 103–4.
See *How to Know the Moon's Phase, 1658.*
Image: John White, *A Rich Cabinet* (1658). Courtesy of the Beinecke Rare Book and Manuscript Library, Yale University.

## How to Make French Toast, 1660:

Robert May, *The Accomplisht Cook, or the Art and Mystery of Cookery* (London, 1660), 162.

Image: Desiderius Erasmus, *Moriæ encomium*, trans. White Kennett (1709). Courtesy of the George Peabody Library, The Sheridan Libraries, Johns Hopkins University.

## How to Make a Giant Egg, 1660:

Robert May, *The Accomplisht Cook*, 427–8.

See *How to Make French Toast, 1660*.

Image: Michael Maier, *Scrutinium chymicum* (1687). Courtesy of the George Peabody Library, The Sheridan Libraries, Johns Hopkins University.

## How to Make a Hedgehog, 1725:

Robert Smith, *Court Cookery: Or, the Compleat English Cook* (London, 1725), 102.

First published in 1723.

Image: Albertus Seba, *Locupletissimi rerum naturalium thesauri accurata descriptio* (1734–65). Courtesy of the George Peabody Library, The Sheridan Libraries, Johns Hopkins University.

## How to Make Ketchup, 1774:

Hannah Glasse, *The Art of Cookery Made Plain and Easy*, 240.

See *How to Make a Christmas Pie, 1774*.

Image: *The Compleat Housewife* (1758). Courtesy of the George Peabody Library, The Sheridan Libraries, Johns Hopkins University.

## How to Make Macaroni and Cheese, c. 1390:

*The Forme of Cury*, trans. Constance B. Hieatt, *The Culinary Recipes of Medieval England: An Epitome of Recipes from Extant Medieval English Culinary Manuscripts* (London, 2013), 91.

*The Forme of Cury (Forms of Cooking)* is an important medieval cookbook, written in Middle English.

Image: Österreichische Nationalbibliothek, Cod. Vindob. series nova 2644, f. 60v.

## How to Make a Pastry Castle, c. 1390:

*The Forme of Cury*, trans. Hieatt, 184.

See *How to Make Macaroni and Cheese, c. 1390*.

Image: The J. Paul Getty Museum, MS Ludwig XIII 3, f. 2v. Image courtesy of the Getty's Open Content Program.

*How to Make a Poisoned Arrow, twelfth century:*

*Mappae clavicula*, ed. and trans. Cyril Stanley Smith and John G. Hawthorne, "*Mappae Clavicula*: A Little Key to the World of Medieval Techniques," *Transactions of the American Philosophical Society* n.s. 64:4 (1974): 1–28, at 68.

The *Mappae clavicula* outlines techniques for a number of crafts. Some of its material dates to antiquity; it continued to receive accretions through the twelfth century.

Image: The J. Paul Getty Museum, MS 46, f. 71r. Image courtesy of the Getty's Open Content Program.

*How to Make a Quick Cocktail, 1658:*

John White, *A Rich Cabinet*, 28.

See *How to Know the Moon's Phase, 1658*.

Image: Hans Holbein, *Simolachri: Historie e figure de la morte* (1549). Courtesy of the George Peabody Library, The Sheridan Libraries, Johns Hopkins University.

*How to Make a Rainbow, 1633:*

Hendrik van Etten [Jean Leurechon?], *Mathematicall Recreations* (London, 1633), 66–8.

This work on mechanical marvels, drawing on Hero of Alexandria, was first published in French in 1624 (*Récréations mathématiques*); it has often been attributed to Jean Leurechon. This is the first English edition.

Image: René Descartes, *Specimina philosophiae* (1650). Courtesy of the George Peabody Library, The Sheridan Libraries, Johns Hopkins University.

*How to Make Snail Bread, 1685:*

Nicolas Lemery, *Modern Curiosities of Art and Nature*, 240–1.

See *How to Cure Gas, 1685*.

Image: Joachim Camerarius, *Symbolorum et emblematum centuriæ quatuor* (1677).

*How to Make Someone Die of Laughter, thirteenth century:*

Richardus Salernitanus, Anatomia, ed. I. Schwarz, *Die Medizinischen Handschriften der K. Universitätsbibliothek im Würzburg* (Würzburg, 1907), 90. (My translation.)

The identity of this Richardus is not clear; the text may be a version of notes from twelfth-century medical teaching in Salerno.

Image: Walters Art Museum, W.51, f. 2r. © Walters Art Museum, used under a Creative Commons Attribution-ShareAlike 3.0 license.

*How to Make Tagliatelle, 1570:*

Bartolomeo Scappi, *Opera*, trans. Scully, 228.

See *How to Cook a Porcupine, 1570.*

Image: Walters Art Museum, W.313, f. 34r. © Walters Art Museum, used under a Creative Commons Attribution-ShareAlike 3.0 license.

*How to Make a Tattoo, 1563:*

Alessio Piemontese [Girolamo Ruscelli?], *The Second Part of the Secretes of Maister Alexis of Piemont*, trans. Ward, 16.

See *How to Dye Your Hair Green, 1563.*

Image: John Bulwer, *Anthropometamorphosis* (1653). Courtesy of the George Peabody Library, The Sheridan Libraries, Johns Hopkins University.

*How to Make a Turf Bench, c. 1305:*

Piero de' Crescenzi, *Liber ruralium commodorum*, trans. Robert G. Calkins, "Piero de' Crescenzi and the Medieval Garden," in Elisabeth B. MacDougall, ed., *Medieval Gardens* (Washington, D.C., 1986), 171.

Crescenzi's *Opus ruralium commodorum* was one of the most important agricultural treatises of medieval Europe.

Image: Beinecke Library, MS 418, f. 45r. Courtesy of the Beinecke Rare Book and Manuscript Library, Yale University.

*How to Make Your Own Lip Balm, 1579:*

Thomas Lupton, *A Thousand Notable Things*, 2.

See *How to Avoid the Plague, 1579.*

Image: Desiderius Erasmus, *Moriæ encomium*, trans. White Kennett (1709). Courtesy of the George Peabody Library, The Sheridan Libraries, Johns Hopkins University.

*How to Make Yourself Invisible, 1560:*

*The Boke of Secretes of Albertus Magnus* (London, 1560), Civ.

The medieval compilation of experimental magic known as the *Secreta Alberti* was attributed spuriously to Albertus Magnus, though perhaps assmbled in the thirteenth century by one of his followers.

Image: The J. Paul Getty Museum, MS Ludwig XV 9, f. 43v. Image courtesy of the Getty's Open Content Program.

*How to Manage Your Nose, 1640:*

Lucas Gracián Dantisco, *Galateo Espagnol*, trans. W[illiam] S[tyle], 10.

See *How to Belch Politely, 1640*.
Image: John Bulwer, *Anthropometamorphosis* (1653). Courtesy of the
George Peabody Library, The Sheridan Libraries, Johns Hopkins
University.

## *How to Mix Drinks for Ladies, 1892:*

William Schmidt, *The Flowing Bowl: When and What to Drink* (New York, 1892),
164.
Image: "The Pretty Barmaid" (c. 1825). Courtesy of the Wellcome Library, London.

## *How to Mouse-Proof Your Cheese, 1581:*

Thomas Hill, *A Briefe and Pleasaunt Treatise, Entituled, Naturall and Artificiall
Conclusions* (London, 1581), Giv.
Hill's "book of secrets" was first published in 1567 or 1568.
Image: Jean Baudoin, *Les fables d'Esope* (1649). Courtesy of the George Peabody
Library, The Sheridan Libraries, Johns Hopkins University.

## *How to Pack for a Journey, 1480:*

Santo Brasca, *Viaggio in Terrasanta*, ed. Anna Laura Momigliano Lepschy, *Viaggio
in Terrasanta di Santo Brasca 1480* (Milan, 1966), 128–9. (My translation.)
*Viaggio in Terrasanta* (*Journey to the Holy Land*) is a day-by-day account of the
Milanese author's pilgrimage to Jerusalem in the year 1480.
Image: The J. Paul Getty Museum, MS Ludwig XIII 7, f. 120v. Image courtesy of
the Getty's Open Content Program.

## *How to Party Like a Scholar, 1558:*

Giovanni della Casa, *Il Galateo overo de' costumi*, trans. M. F. Rusnak, *Galateo: Or,
The Rules of Polite Behavior* (Chicago, 2013), 20.
Archbishop Giovanni della Casa's *Galateo*, first published posthumously in 1558,
quickly became one of the most influential books on manners ever written;
*galateo* is still a byword for good manners in Italian.
Image: Benito Arias Montano, *Humanae salutis monumenta* (1571). Courtesy
of the George Peabody Library, The Sheridan Libraries, Johns Hopkins
University.

## *How to Predict Bad Weather, c. 1470:*

*Les Evangiles des Quenouilles*, trans. Jeay and Garay, 119.
See *How to Keep Your Cat, c. 1470*.
Image: Lyon, Bibliothèque municipale, MS 6881, f. 30r.

*How to Predict Cost of Living, c. 1470:*

*Les Evangiles des Quenouilles*, trans. Jeay and Garay, 129.
See *How to Keep Your Cat, c. 1470.*
Image: Lyon, Bibliothèque municipale, Rés. Inc. 58, f. 43r.

*How to Prepare a Bath, c. 1450:*

John Russell, *Boke of Nurture*, trans. Edith Rickert and L. J. Naylor, *The Babees Book: Medieval Manners for the Young* (Cambridge, ON, 2000), 34.
Little is known about John Russell; he describes himself as an usher, marshal, and servant to Duke Humphrey of Gloucester.
Image: Heidelberg University Library, Cod. Pal. Germ. 848, f. 46v.

*How to Prevent Back Pain, c. 1470:*

*Les Evangiles des Quenouilles*, trans. Jeay and Garay, 211.
See *How to Keep Your Cat, 1470.*
Image: Österreichische Nationalbibliothek, Cod. Vindob. series nova 2644, f. 37r.

*How to Prevent Drunkenness, 1653:*

Hugh Plat, *The Jewel House of Art and Nature* (London, 1653), 59.
Image: Thomas Heywood, *Philocothonista* (1635). Courtesy of the Beinecke Rare Book and Manuscript Library, Yale University.

*How to Protect Your Infant, 1697:*

John Pechey, *A General Treatise of the Diseases of Infants and Children Collected from the Best Practical Authors* (London, 1697), 4–5.
Image: Richard Mead, *A Mechanical Account of Poisons in Several Essays* (1745). Courtesy of the Wellcome Library, London.

*How to Put the Moves on a Man, c. 1250:*

Richard de Fournival, *Consaus d'amours*, trans. Norman R. Shapiro, *The Comedy of Eros: Medieval French Guides to the Art of Love*, 2nd ed. (Urbana, IL, 1997), 116.
Better known for his *Bestiaire d'amour* (*Bestiary of Love*), Richard de Fournival also composed an epistolary treatise on love.
Image: British Library, Stowe MS 17, f. 145r. © The British Library Board.

*How to Put Out a Fire, twelfth century:*

*Mappae clavicula*, trans. Smith and Hawthorne, 70.
See *How to Make a Poisoned Arrow, twelfth century.*

Image: The J. Paul Getty Museum, MS Ludwig XIV 6, f. 126r. Image courtesy of
the Getty's Open Content Program.

*How to Raise Your Child, twelfth century:*

*The Trotula*, trans. Green, 109.
See *How to Avoid Pregnancy, twelfth century.*
Image: Morgan Library, MS G.24, f. 10r. Jacques de Longuyon, *Les voeux du paon*,
c. 1350. Gift of the Trustees of the William S. Glazier Collection, 1984. The
Pierpont Morgan Library, New York/Art Resource, NY.

*How to Recover from a Dance Mishap, 1538:*

Antonius Arena, *Leges dansandi.* (My translation.)
See *How to Dress for Dancing, 1538.*
Image: Cesare Negri, *Nuove inventioni di balli* (1604). Courtesy of the Beinecke
Rare Book and Manuscript Library, Yale University.

*How to Relieve Yourself, c. 1200:*

Daniel of Beccles, *Urbanus magnus*, 38–9. (My translation.)
See *How to Dress Your Child, c. 1200.*
Image: Bodleian Library, MS Bodl. 264 pt. 1, f. 56r. By permission of the Bodleian
Library, University of Oxford.

*How to Remove a Stain, 1562:*

Alessio Piemontese [Girolamo Ruscelli?], *The Thyrde and Last Parte of the Secretes of
the Reverende Maister Alexis of Piemont*, trans. William Ward (London, 1562), 58.
See *How to Dye Your Hair Green, 1563.*
Image: Matthias de L'Obel, *Kruydtboeck* (1581). Courtesy of the Wellcome Library,
London.

*How to Ride a Horse, c. 1260:*

Brunetto Latini, *Il Tesoretto*, ed. Julia Bolton Holloway, *Il Tesoretto* (*The Little
Treasure*) (New York, 1981), 1803–18. (My translation.)
Brunetto Latini is best known as Dante's mentor and for his appearance among
the sodomites in Dante's *Inferno.* Latini sought to summarize all of human
knowledge in his Italian poem *Tesoretto* and French prose *Li Livres dou Trésor.*
Image: British Library, Stowe MS 17, f. 153v. © The British Library Board.

*How to Serve a Live Bird at a Feast, c. 1450:*

*The Vivendier*, trans. Scully, 81.

See *How to Make a Cooked Bird Sing, c. 1450.*
Image: Bodleian Library, MS Bodl. 264 pt. 1, f. 73v. By permission of the Bodleian
   Library, University of Oxford.

## *How to Serve Wine to Your Toddler, c. 1450:*

Michele Savonarola, *Ad mulieres ferrarienses.* (My translation.)
See *How to Give Birth, c. 1450.*
Image: Österreichische Nationalbibliothek, Cod. Vindob. series nova 2644, f. 85v.

## *How to Sing, 1650:*

Christoph Bernhard, *Von der Singe-Kunst oder Manier,* trans. Walter Hilse, "The
   Treatises of Christoph Bernhard," *The Music Forum* III (1973), 25.
Bernhard's advice on singing exists in a manuscript from around 1650.
Image: Hans Sachs, *Eygentliche Beschreibung aller Stände auff Erden* (1568). Courtesy
   of the Beinecke Rare Book and Manuscript Library, Yale University.

## *How to Sit at the Table, 1530:*

Desiderius Erasmus, *De civilitate,* 28. (My translation.)
See *How to Fart, 1530.*
Image: Girolamo Mercuriale, *De arte gymnastica* (1601). Courtesy of the George
   Peabody Library, The Sheridan Libraries, Johns Hopkins University.

## *How to Sleep, 1474:*

Platina, *De honesta voluptate et valetudine,* trans. Milham, 111.
See *How to Choose a Cook, 1474.*
Image: Österreichische Nationalbibliothek, Cod. Vindob. series nova 2644, f. 101v.

## *How to Sleep While Traveling, 1700:*

Andrew Balfour, *Letters Write* [sic] *to a Friend* (Edinburgh, 1700), 111.
This set of letters from the physician, botanist, and traveler Andrew Balfour to
   Patrick Murray were published after Balfour's death in 1694.
Image: Johann Theodor de Bry, *India orientalis* (1598). Courtesy of the George
   Peabody Library, The Sheridan Libraries, Johns Hopkins University.

## *How to Slim Down in Fourteen Days, 1579:*

Thomas Lupton, *A Thousand Notable Things,* 49.
See *How to Avoid the Plague, 1579.*
Image: John Bulwer, *Anthropometamorphosis* (1653). Courtesy of the George
   Peabody Library, The Sheridan Libraries, Johns Hopkins University.

*How to Sober Up*, 1612:

*The Booke of Pretty Conceits: Taken out of Latine, French, Dutch and English* (London, 1628), A7v.

Image: Johann Dryander, *Der gantzen Artzenei* (1542). Courtesy of the Wellcome Library, London.

*How to Soothe a Child*, c. 1000:

*Old English Herbarium*, trans. Anne van Arsdall, *Medieval Herbal Remedies: The Old English Herbarium and Anglo-Saxon Medicine* (New York, 2002), 159.

A translation into Old English of a fourth- or fifth-century Latin compilation known as the *Herbarium of Pseudo-Apuleius*.

Image: Bodleian Library, MS Junius 11, p. 53. By permission of the Bodleian Library, University of Oxford.

*How to Soothe a Teething Baby*, c. 1450:

Michele Savonarola, *Ad mulieres ferrarienses*. (My translation.)

See *How to Give Birth, c. 1450*.

Image: Bodleian Library, MS Douce 276, f. 118r. By permission of the Bodleian Library, University of Oxford.

*How to Spit*, 1646:

Francis Hawkins, *Youths Behaviour*, 7.

See *How to Converse, 1646*.

Image: Richard Brathwaite, *The English Gentleman* (1630). Courtesy of the Beinecke Rare Book and Manuscript Library, Yale University.

*How to Stay Healthy*, 1607:

John Harrington, *The Englishmans Docter, or the School of Salerne* (London, 1607), A8r.

A verse translation of the *Regimen sanitatis Salernitanum*.

Image: John Gerard, *The Herball or Generall Historie of Plantes* (1633). Courtesy of the George Peabody Library, The Sheridan Libraries, Johns Hopkins University.

*How to Stay Young*, 1489:

Marsilio Ficino, *De vita libri tres*, ed. and trans. Carol V. Kaske and John R. Clarke, *Three Books on Life* (Binghamton, NY, 1989), 197.

Marsilio Ficino, known for translating Plato into Latin, explored more esoteric interests in his *Tres libri de vita* (*Three Books on Life*) of 1489, including ways to harness positive influences from the stars.

Image: Abraham Bosse, "Anchora Inparo" (1538). Courtesy of the Wellcome
    Library, London.

*How to Sweet-Talk Your Lady*, 1656:

*Cupids Master-piece, or, the Free-school of Witty and Delightful Complements* (London,
    1656).
Image: *The Young-mans Unfortunate Destiny* (1684–95?). Courtesy of the Beinecke
    Rare Book and Manuscript Library, Yale University.

*How to Swim Like a Man*, 1860:

Donald Walker, *Walker's Manly Exercises: Containing Rowing, Sailing, Riding,
    Driving, Hunting, Shooting, and Other Manly Sports*, rev. 'Craven' (London, 1860), 86.
Image: Donald Walker, *Walker's Manly Exercises* (1860). Courtesy of the George
    Peabody Library, The Sheridan Libraries, Johns Hopkins University.

*How to Talk about Your Kids*, 1558:

Giovanni della Casa, *Il Galateo overo de' costumi*, trans. Rusnak, 48–9.
See *How to Party Like a Scholar, 1558.*
Image: Paolo Veronese, *Giuseppe da Porto and His Son Adriano.* Galleria degli Uffizi,
    Firenze. HIP/Art Resource, NY.]

*How to Tell Jokes*, 1558:

Giovanni della Casa, *Il Galateo overo de' costumi*, trans. Rusnak, 47.
See *How to Party Like a Scholar, 1558.*
Image: Wenceslaus Hollar, *Portrait of Giovanni della Casa.* Courtesy of the Thomas
    Fisher Rare Book Library, University of Toronto.

*How to Tell if Someone Is or Is Not Dead*, c. 1380:

Johannes de Mirfield, *Breviarium Bartholomei*, trans. Percival Horton-Smith
    Hartley and Harold Richard Aldridge, *Johannes de Mirfeld of St. Bartholomew's,
    Smithfield; His Life and Works* (Cambridge, 1936), 69.
John of Mirfield was an eminent physician at St. Bartholomew's Hospital
    (London); two copies of his practical medical compendium survive.
Image: The J. Paul Getty Museum, MS Ludwig XIII 7, f. 159v. Image courtesy of
    the Getty's Open Content Program.

*How to Tell Time*, 1658:

John White, *A Rich Cabinet*, 8.
See *How to Know the Moon's Phase, 1658.*

Image: Pliny the Elder, *Historia mundi naturalis* (1582). Courtesy of the George
Peabody Library, The Sheridan Libraries, Johns Hopkins University.

## *How to Train Your Cat to Do Tricks, 1809:*

Jesse Haney, *Haney's Art of Training Animals* (New York, 1809), 148–9.
Image: *Dame Wiggins of Lee and Her Seven Wonderful Cats* (1836). Courtesy
of the George Peabody Library, The Sheridan Libraries, Johns Hopkins
University.

## *How to Train Your Sparrow Hawk, c. 1393:*

*Le Ménagier de Paris*, trans. Greco and Rose, 237–8.
See *How to Care for Your Dog, c. 1393.*
Image: Morgan Library, MS M.144, f. 4r. Book of Hours, c. 1490. Purchased by J.
Pierpont Morgan before 1913. The Pierpont Morgan Library, New York/Art
Resource, NY.

## *How to Treat Baldness, thirteenth century:*

Salvatore de Renzi, *Collectio Salernitana*, vol. 5 (Naples, 1859), 21. (My translation.)
Image: British Library Royal 6 E VII, f. 197r. © The British Library Board.

## *How to Treat Freshmen, 1495:*

Leipzig University statute, ed. Friedrich Zarncke, *Die Statutenbücher der Universität
Leipzig* (Leipzig, 1861), 102, trans. Robert Francis Seybolt, *The Manuale
Scholarium: An Original Account of Life in the Mediaeval University* (Cambridge,
MA, 1921), 21–2, n. 6. (Translation slightly adapted.)
Image: Laurentius de Voltolina, "The Classroom of Henricus de Alemannia,"
c. 1360–90. bpk, Berlin/Kupferstichkabinett, Staatliche Museen, Berlin/Joerg
P. Anders/Art Resource, NY.

## *How to Trim Your Toenails Underwater, 1789:*

Melchisédech Thévenot, *The Art of Swimming. Illustrated by Forty Proper Copper-
Plate Cuts, Which Represent the Different Postures Necessary to be Used in that Art.
With Advice for Bathing*, 3rd ed. (London, 1789), 47–8.
Thévenot's *L'Art de Nager*, first published in 1696, was a French version of Everard
Digby's Latin manual *De arte natandi* (1587), translated from French to English
in 1699 and still dispensing good advice about aquatic grooming in 1789.
Image: Melchisédech Thévenot, *The Art of Swimming* (1789). Courtesy of the
George Peabody Library, The Sheridan Libraries, Johns Hopkins
University.

*How to Turn Down Your Lord's Wife, c. 1200:*

Daniel of Beccles, *Urbanus magnus*, 64. (My translation.)
See *How to Dress Your Child, c. 1200.*
Image: Walters Art Museum, W.106, f. 15r. © Walters Art Museum, used under a
    Creative Commons Attribution-ShareAlike 3.0 license.

*How to Use Bacon, c. 530:*

Anthimus, *De obseruatione ciborum*, ed. and trans. Mark Grant (Totnes, 1996), 57.
*De obseruatione ciborum* (*On the Observance of Foods*) is the work of a Byzantine
    physician at the court of Theodoric the Great.
Image: The J. Paul Getty Museum, MS 100, f. 26v. Image courtesy of the Getty's
    Open Content Program.

*How to Use an Orange, 1722:*

Joseph Miller, *Botanicum officinale: or a Compendious Herbal* (London, 1722),
    67–8.
Image: Elizabeth Blackwell, *Herbarium Blackwellianum* (1757). Courtesy of the
    Beinecke Rare Book and Manuscript Library, Yale University.

*How to Wake or Sleep, 1685:*

Nicolas Lemery, *Modern Curiosities of Art and Nature*, 26.
See *How to Cure Gas, 1685.*
Image: Conrad Gesner, *Historiae animalium* (1551). Courtesy of the George
    Peabody Library, The Sheridan Libraries, Johns Hopkins University.

*How to Walk on Water, 1581:*

Thomas Hill, *A Briefe and Pleasaunt Treatise, Entituled, Naturall and Artificiall
    Conclusions*, C5r.
See *How to Mouse-Proof Your Cheese, 1649.*
Image: Thomas Hill, *Naturall and Artificiall Conclusions* (1649). Courtesy of the
    Beinecke Rare Book and Manuscript Library, Yale University.

*How to Wash a Baby, 1744:*

Thomas Dawkes, *The Nurse's Guide: or, Short and Safer Rules for the Management of
    Women* (London, 1744), 35–6.
Image: *Aristotle's Works Compleated* (1733). Courtesy of the Wellcome Library,
    London.

*How to Wash Your Hair, twelfth century:*

*The Trotula*, trans. Green, 171.
See *How to Avoid Pregnancy, twelfth century.*
Image: The J. Paul Getty Museum, MS 100, f. 58r. Image courtesy of the Getty's Open Content Program.

*How to Wash Your Head, 1612:*

William Vaughan, *Approved Directions for Health* (London, 1612), 71.
First published in 1600.
Image: Girolamo Mercuriale, *De arte gymnastica* (1601). Courtesy of the George Peabody Library, The Sheridan Libraries, Johns Hopkins University.

*How to Wear Gentlemanly Underwear, 1891:*

Mortimer Delano de Lannoy, *Simplex Munditiis. Gentlemen* (New York, 1891), 55.
Image: *The Underwear and Hosiery Review* 1, no. 4 (February, 1918). Courtesy of the Milton S. Eisenhower Library, The Sheridan Libraries, Johns Hopkins University.

*How to Wear Platform Shoes, 1600:*

Fabritio Caroso, *Nobiltà di dame*, ed. and trans. Julia Sutton, *Courtly Dance of the Renaissance: A New Translation and Edition of the* Nobiltà di Dame *(1600)* (New York, 1995), 141.
The dance master Fabritio Caroso da Sermoneta first published *Il Ballarino* in 1584; *Nobiltà di dame* is a revision.
Image: John Bulwer, *Anthropometamorphosis* (1653). Courtesy of the George Peabody Library, The Sheridan Libraries, Johns Hopkins University

*How to Whiten Your Teeth, 1686:*

Hannah Woolley, *The Accomplish'd Ladies Delight*, 95.
See *How to Heal All Wounds, 1686.*
Image: Hans Sachs, *Eygentliche Beschreibung aller Stände auff Erden* (1568). Courtesy of the Beinecke Rare Book and Manuscript Library, Yale University.

*How to Win a Legal Case, c. 1260:*

Albertus Magnus, *De animalibus*, trans. Kitchell and Resnick, 1520.
See *How to Care for Your Cat, c. 1260.*
Image: British Library, Royal MS 6 E VI, f. 128v. © The British Library Board.